Humanism and Environmentalism

American University Studies

Series XIV
Education

Vol. 24

PETER LANG
New York • Washington, D.C./Baltimore • San Francisco
Bern • Frankfurt am Main • Berlin • Vienna • Paris

James E. Nowlin and
J. Vernon Blackburn

Humanism and Environmentalism

Philosophical Perspectives in Counseling

PETER LANG
New York • Washington, D.C./Baltimore • San Francisco
Bern • Frankfurt am Main • Berlin • Vienna • Paris

Library of Congress Cataloging-in-Publication Data

Nowlin, James E.
Humanism and environmentalism: philosophical perspectives in counseling/
James E. Nowlin, J. Vernon Blackburn.
p. cm. — (American university studies. Series XIV, Education; vol. 24)
Includes bibliographical references.
1. Counseling. 2. Humanistic psychology. 3. Behaviorism (Psychology).
I. Blackburn, J. Vernon. II. Title. III. Series.
BF637.C6N68 158′.3—dc20 93-44078
ISBN 0-8204-1109-4
ISSN 0740-4565

Die Deutsche Bibliothek-CIP-Einheitsaufnahme

Nowlin, James E.:
Humanism and environmentalism: philosophical perspectives in counseling/
James E. Nowlin; J. Vernon Blackburn. – New York; Washington, D.C./
Baltimore; San Francisco; Bern; Frankfurt am Main;
Berlin; Vienna; Paris: Lang.
(American university studies: Ser. 14, Education; Vol. 24)
ISBN 0-8204-1109-4
NE: Blackburn, J. Vernon:; American university studies / 14

Dedication

This book is dedicated in loving memory to my father, James W. Nowlin. His support and his love are greatly missed! Additionally, this book is dedicated to Ms. Louise Nowlin, my mother. Her continued patience, encouragement and love are appreciated.

The supreme end of education is expert discernment in all things—the power to tell the good from the bad, the genuine from the counterfeit, and to prefer the good and the genuine to the bad and the counterfeit.

Samuel Johnson

Metaphysics is a dark ocean without shores or lighthouse, strewn with many a philosophic wreck.

I. Kant

It is impossible to escape the impression that people commonly use false standards of measurements—that they seek power, success and wealth for themselves and admire them in others, and that they often underestimate what is of true value in life.

Sigmund Freud

Science without religion is lame, religion without science is blind.

Albert Einstein

If 50 million people say a foolish thing, it is still a foolish thing.

Anatole France

I never give them hell. I just tell the truth and they think it's hell.

Harry S. Truman

For Man was a culture-bearer as well as a soul-bearer, but his cultures were not immortal and they could die with a race or an age, and then human reflections of meaning and human portrayals of truth receded, and truth and meaning resided, unseen, only in the objective logos of Nature and the ineffable Logos of God. Truth could be crucified; but soon, perhaps, a resurrection.

Walter M. Miller, *A Canticle for Leibowitz*

Acknowledgment

This book could not have been produced without the financial and moral support of the Montana State University-Billings Foundation. The authors would like to express their sincere gratitude to the Foundation for its involvement.

Contents

I The Historical Context of Humanism Versus Environmentalism 1

II The Relationship of Humanism to Metaphysics and Environmentalism to Antimetaphysics 37

III Fundamental Principles of Humanism and Environmentalism 51

IV B. F. Skinner 101

V Viktor Frankl 123

VI Summary 143

Bibliography 159

Chapter I

The Historical Context of Humanism Versus Environmentalism

It has become increasingly clear that there are considerably more points of contention and diversity than agreement in the present field of counseling theory. Carl Rogers (1963) referred to the chaotic and divided nature of the field and how this divisiveness is not superficial but is apparent at the most basic levels of counseling thought. Colley (1970) noted that the different theoretical stances taken by the so-called major counseling movements (behavioral, existential, psychoanalytic, and others) differ on almost every important point. These differences include definitions and methodology. On the other hand, the single agreement in the profession is limited to the recognition that counseling should attempt to provide a service designed to achieve some helping purpose. Other scholars within the field have long commented on the depth of the differences in counseling theory and practice. Theoreticians have often examined these differences on both a theoretical and practical plane. However, few people have looked at the basic philosophical assumptions which form the foundations of the major counseling theories. The intent of this writing is to examine counseling conflicts at the most fundamental level, the level of metaphysical inquiry.

The importance of studying the differing metaphysical bases underlying various movements of counseling thought is readily apparent when one considers that in practice most counselors consciously affiliate themselves with one movement or another and choose one theoretical stance over others. One study (White, 1978) found that over 90% of the counselors participating in the research study were easily identified with distinct theoretical stances. The importance of this cannot be overstated. Accepting the tenets of one particular theory over others puts one in the position of stating that this theory has more worth or is more valid (at least to that person) than other theories. If there is any correlation between theory and metaphysical assumptions, this puts one in the position of accepting certain of these assumptions and rejecting others.

Although there are any number of specific counseling theories, fundamentally there are two major forces dominating modern counseling thought. For purposes of convenience and identification, Barclay (1971) called these oppositional movements humanism and environmentalism. In order to promote a sense of internal consistency, these labels will be used throughout this book.

Environmentalism is understood to be a general category made up of all those theories commonly called behavioral. Humanism is a less distinct movement and is often referred to as counseling's "third force." Its major emphasis is on the importance of each individual as a unique personal self. From a strictly methodological standpoint, the various theories subsumed in this category agree on only two points: a general opposition to environmental theories and methods, and a strong consistency in their basic metaphysical structure. In addition to the attempt to identify and clarify the philosophical assumptions underlying these two very different streams of counseling thought, the attempt will also be made to trace the metaphysical perspectives which gave birth to these fundamental counseling assumptions.

The task of discussing the nature and scope of any branch of knowledge is difficult, "but the difficulty is exceptionally great in the case of the body of investigations traditionally known as metaphysics" (Taylor, 1903, p. 1). Rendering the problem of metaphysics especially difficult is the modern prejudice which regards metaphysics as nonexistent and its problems as illusory (Taylor, 1903). In dealing with these difficulties, only two courses are open to selection: answering the questions haphazardly as it suits a momentary caprice or answering them on intelligible principles (Taylor, 1903). The choice of the latter of these two courses clearly means that before any conclusions can be formulated, a systematic and impartial inquiry into the familiar distinction of what merely "seems" and what really "is" must be undertaken. In other words, what is required is

> a scientific inquiry into the general characteristics by which reality or real being is distinguished from mere appearance, not in some special sphere of study, but universally. (Taylor, 1903, p. 4)

Such an inquiry is precisely what is meant by metaphysics. Metaphysics is thus understood to be the fundamental philosophic assumption that makes "the attempt to find the right intellectual attitude toward ultimate reality" (Taylor, 1903, p. xii).

The major thrust of this book is the investigation of the philosophical assumptions underlying the two most current forces in counseling theory, humanism and environmentalism. The fact that these two positions are philosophically opposed lies at the heart of the modern conflict and divergence in both counseling theory and practice.

Counseling will not resolve or even understand this conflict if it persists in attacking the issue on the basis of theories, practices, or methodologies. Understanding begins where the problems begin. In the case of counseling, this beginning is the philosophical assumptions and the metaphysical context from which these assumptions are born. Counseling seems to have fallen into the trap of acute tunnel vision. When it examines its own conflicts, it invariably does so only in terms of procedural questions and rarely, if ever, does it consider the relationship of procedure to opposing conceptions of ultimate reality. For instance, counseling usually considers the humanism-environmentalism conflict as simple questions of method (counselor manipulation versus nonmanipulation, for example) or theory (Rogerian theory versus Skinnerian theory). Few within the field (James R. Barclay is a notable exception) have approached the humanism-environmentalism conflict at a more basic starting point, the ontological, epistemological, and axiological differences which form the crux of the problem. (These terms are being used here in their traditional philosophic meanings. Ontology is the investigation of being or reality, epistemology denotes those investigations dealing specifically with the process of knowing, and axiology deals with the study of value orientations). By using and building on Barclay's work in the area of counseling philosophy, the attempt will be made to: (a) establish a relationship between counseling's humanist-environmentalist conflict and the broader philosophic conflict of metaphysics versus antimetaphysics; (b) clarify this issue for counselors by approaching it through metaphysical analysis in order to try to bring philosophic clarity and engender philosophic inquiry in counseling; (c) identify and clarify the major philosophical assumptions underlying two dominant forces in modern counseling thought (humanism and environmentalism); and (d) examine certain metaphysical concepts (ultimate realities) in the writings of a specific representative theorist on each side of the counseling debate in order to gauge the effect of these concepts on counseling theories, and, to a lesser degree, counseling practices.

Most philosophers are keenly aware of the debate between metaphysicians and antimetaphysicians. The philosophical literature is often dominated by this centuries-old conflict. The earlier reference to counseling's tunnel vision is premised on the fact that many of those involved in counseling are oblivious to this philosophical debate as well as to the profound impact that this conflict has on their own field. While this study makes no claim that it will resolve the conflict over metaphysics, the reasons for examining this issue are threefold: (a) to remediate the lack of philosophical grounding within counseling theory; (b) to acquaint those counselors who are unaware of this issue with the metaphysical-antimetaphysical debate; (c) to attempt to show a relationship between the philosophical conflict and the humanist-environmentalist conflict in counseling and to bring greater sophistication to counseling by examining the effect that the philosophical debate might have on the counseling debate.

It is with a considerable amount of certainty that one could say that the concept of general philosophical assumptions in the field of counseling has been, and is now, the most neglected aspect of the counseling movement. In his book, *Philosophical Foundations of Guidance*, Carlton Beck (1963) lamented this state of affairs and also proposed several reasons to explain how and why this came to be. He pointed to the rapid growth of guidance, especially in its formative years, as one of the main reasons why the field of counseling has been so long without "a carefully unified theory and scholarly detailed statement of philosophical foundations" (p. 3). In counseling the emphasis, from the beginning, has always been geared toward the elimination of some immediate problem. Arbuckle (1965) noted that this quest for immediacy in counseling's formative stages has resulted in "far too many counselors who do not know what they are doing, and an even larger number who do not appear to have a very good understanding of why they are doing what they are doing or what they think they are doing" (p. 49). Another reason for the lack of emphasis on the philosophical aspects of counseling according to Beck (1963) has been the fact that for most of its history counseling has been geared toward treating specific symptoms instead of an in-depth analysis of itself as a field of study. Counseling literature reflects this preoccupation with symptomology and methodology.

Collingwood (1940) noted that almost any science's study of itself revealed a paradox. The practices and methodologies are born out of the universals, i.e., the philosophical assumptions of the particular science. In other words, the practices, methods, and specific recommendations for treating symptoms (or questions, depending on the science) come after the universals have been decided upon. Yet in order of study, the practices and methods precede the universals. Counseling assuredly follows this form. A look at almost any college curriculum in counseling will reveal that, in order of study, counseling techniques are taught early in the program. A few curricula will also have a detailed investigation of counseling theory taught later, but most counseling curricula fail to consider the implications of the philosophical assumptions underlying both theory and practice. Perhaps initially this happens in every field of study, but eventually an examination of the universals which give birth to the particulars of a science must be investigated. Unlike most other fields, counseling has long neglected this investigation and continues to concentrate primarily on practices and methods, a trend which is naturally reflected in counseling literature. As of 1951 only one doctoral dissertation, by Cribben (1951), made any attempt to deal chiefly with the philosophical issues of counseling. "Cribben was the first to examine and summarize the philosophical assumptions reflected in the guidance movement's literature" (Colley, 1970, p. 3). In the past three decades there has been a noticeable increase of interest in the philosophic issues of counseling, but this increase could hardly be called a renaissance within the field. During this time only two books, both by Barclay, have attempted to identify the specific philosophical assumptions from which counseling theories and practices have been formulated. Even these excellent texts stop short of attempting to delineate the relationship of these assumptions to specific counseling theorists.

Yet, while on one hand one sees this paucity of study concerning the philosophical principles of guidance, on the other hand one also notes the fact that many respected people in the field continue to assert the importance and need for such studies. They seem agreed that it will mainly be through the use of philosophical constructs that counseling will move beyond common sense. "Every scientific method rests on philosophical presuppositions" (May, 1967, p. 8). "Every learning theorist [one could substitute counseling theorist] is a philosopher though he may not know it" (Allport, 1961, p. 84). "The 'why' of counseling is the philosophical rationale for whatever one does as a counselor [theory and method]" (Arbuckle, 1965, p. 3). "Philosophical inquiry results in values of importance and worth, affording a vision of ends towards which counseling as a means should be directed" (Barclay, 1971, p. 21). These are certainly questions and statements that should concern counseling. They are also ontological, epistemological, and axiological concerns. They are concerns about ultimate reality, and, as such, they can be dealt with by counseling only in a philosophic context. This makes counseling's paradox complete. Most agree that counseling has philosophical assumptions, and many within the field speak of the necessity for coming to grips with these assumptions. Yet in actual practice counseling philosophy exists as a virtual desert.

Collingwood (1940) insisted that every field of science exists in the form of a triumvirate. There are philosophical assumptions (metaphysical presuppositions or metatheory), theory (the basic tenets of a science), and practice (the utilization of theory). Theory is formed on the foundational supports of philosophical assumptions, and specific practices are determined by whatever theoretical stance a field of study adopts. All of these elements are crucial to the life and continued growth of any field of study. Practice without theory is purposeless busywork. Theory without a superstructure of philosophical assumptions is very much like a house lacking a foundation. It may have an imposing facade, but in reality it is inconsequential and without meaning. Each element has its place, and no science, no field of inquiry, can reach its full potential if it chooses to ignore any one of these parts. This seems especially true in the case of philosophic assumptions because this is the starting point of any field of study.

> If a man, while pursuing or expounding a science, makes a mistake as to its nature or the nature of its subject matter, it is quite possible that this mistake will infect all his later work with a certain amount of error. (Collingwood, 1940, p. 17)

Arbuckle (1965), in his book *Counseling: Philosophy, Theory and Practice,* made this same argument. He stated that the first question to be asked is *why* we do what we do, not *what* we do. The answer to this *why* can only come from the philosophical assumptions on which theory and practice rest.

> The preliminary basic responsibility of any professional worker is to come to some understanding of the basic purpose of the professional activity that he plans to enter. Failure to examine these basic responsibilities, which find their genesis in philosophic assumptions, inevitably leads to professional workers who can give no better reason than "just because" for their professional activity. (p. 50)

If the work of the counselor is valuable, then its value must be intelligently defensible. If counseling rests solely on the "just because" defense, it can only be a pseudoscience and can never reach its full professional potential. The defense and propagation of counseling must begin with a concentrated effort to understand the basic philosophic assumptions that form its foundation. The dearth of material in the literature and in the classrooms where future counselors are taught overwhelmingly indicates that the philosophy of counseling still exists as something of a poor stepchild in relation to the work being done in counseling methodology and practice.

Those counselors who seek to understand their field by studying psychological theories are proceeding in the proper direction, but they often make a crucial error in that they stop their investigations at the level of theory instead of continuing on to more fundamental levels of examination. The fundamental assumptions forming the basic foundations of counseling begin, not with psychological theory, but rather with philosophy. Barclay, Rogers, Maritain, Frankl, and other respected members of the field of counseling agree that the future prosperity of counseling will depend on achieving a fundamental understanding of the ontological, epistemological, and axiological implications inherent in counseling thought.

The implications to counseling of these metaphysical concepts and the implications of metaphysics to philosophy in general are quite similar. In each case there exists a situation of basic polarity; one group defending metaphysics and an oppositional force denying its importance and even in some cases its very existence. Historically examining the debate between metaphysicians and the so-called antimetaphysicians is significant to this present study because it will serve to acquaint counselors with this argument and, more importantly, because this centuries-old philosophic conflict has a definite impact on the modern counseling conflict of humanism versus environmentalism.

Those defending metaphysics see it in terms of universal applicability, with propositions drawn from particular instances of reality which can be assigned universal scope. Those denying metaphysics see it as a confusion of simple procedural questions (Bradley, 1908). This is no small disagreement or mere semantical issue. Whether one accepts or rejects metaphysics determines the positions to be taken on the most fundamental questions of ontology, epistemology, and axiology. In large part, these positions are not reconcilable. Aristotle (cited in Drennen, 1962) wrote that metaphysics is the universal science which deals with the ultimate principles of whatever is or can be. In *The Structure of Metaphysics*, Morris Lazerowitz (1955) conversely stated that metaphysics is the pursuit of nonsensical statements and problems. Furthermore, he claimed that those who practice metaphysics are ill from their own words and that they dream incessantly about impossible feats of cognition. The distance between the ultimate principles of Aristotle's metaphysics and Lazerowitz's contempt for metaphysics as verbal nonsense is great. There is no known bridge for this deep philosophic chasm. It remains largely an either/or position with precious few points of commonality or compromise.

A point-by-point examination of each argument and counterargument in the metaphysics-antimetaphysics controversy would represent a lifetime effort and certainly lies beyond the scope and intent of this present writing. But the attempt will be made to trace a relationship between the counseling controversy and the broader philosophic controversy and also to examine the most general and universal arguments on each side of the philosophic debate in order to obtain an historically accurate picture of the relationship between the counseling and philosophic conflicts.

The first antimetaphysical argument to be devised was the contention that there was no such thing as metaphysics. This antimetaphysical argument is first and foremost an analysis of being and knowledge of being. The argument that metaphysics does not exist is usually based on the conclusion that metaphysical truths are

> supposed to be supernatural, or in some way divorced from the immediately observable world of nature. These are precisely the statements where the most difficulty about meaning and verification arise. (Wilson, 1969, pp. 81–82)

The argument states that great sages, saints, mystics, and moralists have attempted to unveil the truths of metaphysics and yet humankind as a whole seems to be nowhere near understanding such truths. To put it simply, metaphysics is dismissed because meaning and being are synonymous, and if there is no possible method of verification then there can be no meaning and, hence, no intelligible discussion of being (Wilson, 1969). Any metaphysical or a priori propositions owe their certainty to the fact that they are tautologies.

> We may accordingly define a metaphysical sentence as a sentence which purports to express a genuine proposition, but does, in fact, express neither a tautology nor an empirical hypothesis. And as tautologies and empirical hypotheses form the entire class of significant propositions, we are justified in concluding that all metaphysical assertions are nonsensical. (Ayer, 1945, p. 38)

Thus, in terms of legitimate contributions, metaphysical statements also have to be considered nonexistent as well as nonsensical.

This line of thought is highly specious even to those philosophers who basically distrust metaphysics. Wilson (1969) admitted that rather than being classified as nonexistent or nonsensical, a metaphysical statement "is like putting a letter in a 'pending' tray: it means that we do not yet know what it means or how to verify it, and that therefore we must reserve judgment about whether it is true or not" (p. 70). F.H. Bradley was willing to go much further in defending the existence of metaphysics. In *Appearances and Reality* Bradley (1908) noted a crippling ambiguity in this antimetaphysical argument. He said that those denying the existence of metaphysics were not actually antimetaphysicians; rather, they were "brother metaphysicians" who merely espouse rival metaphysical systems. He further contended that the effort to disprove metaphysics must of necessity turn itself into a metaphysical analysis of meaning. In denying it, one is, by definition, claiming to pronounce on the character of knowledge and reality. This in turn demands an antecedent knowledge of what reality is, and this is precisely what metaphysical inquiry is all about. Bradley (1908) stated that those who deny metaphysics' existence actually say nothing about whether or not it exists. Their argument is not based on existence but rather on the idea of what metaphysical system should be given credence.

Rudolph Carnap (1957) attempted to rebut Bradley's line of reasoning and proposed a second major argument against metaphysics. Carnap suggested that one could "give in" to Bradley's logic and acknowledge that it is theoretically possible for metaphysical knowledge to exist. But that in no way alters the fact that such knowledge is useless and results only in barrenness and confusion. It generates the same problems, the same disputes, and the same failures. Given this, why not abandon it?

Metaphysicians contend that this argument has value only if one equates the term imperfection with worthless. They claim that if one is to insist, as Carnap seems to, that metaphysics should be abandoned because of its inexactitude, then one must also be willing to abandon all science for that same reason. No one argues the fact that metaphysical issues are difficult. These expressional difficulties are bound to involve problems of meaning. But those supporting metaphysics hold that to choose silence because there is not universal and absolute clarity in every metaphysical discussion is to choose a false alternative. "For a proposition is never untrue simply because it is not the whole truth, but only when, not being the whole truth, it is mistakenly taken to be so" (Taylor, 1903, p. 214). The claim for the worth of knowledge, even though partial in nature, is reinforced over and over in science. Metaphysicians claim that an example of the worth of partial knowledge can be found in elementary mathematics. It is known what the term "pi" stands for. "It is completely determined for us by the definition that it is the ratio of the circumference of a circle to its diameter" (Taylor, 1903, p. 37). The knowledge of the symbol is clear, but the knowledge of pi, though final, is imperfect. The quantity of pi is incommensurable. It can never be precisely evaluated. A value is assigned to it within a degree of approximation. No approximation is more than approximately true, but it does not follow that all approximations are equally wide of the mark. Some approximations are valuable because, while still approximations, they are nearer the truth than others (Taylor, 1903). Metaphysicians argue that denying metaphysics because its knowledge is incomplete would be as much an error as denying all of science because of its incomplete knowledge.

The idea that metaphysical speculation is or is not worthwhile provides the impetus for another area of conflict. This concern is based on the principle of utility. The general nature of the utility question can be stated in terms of a challenge by the antimetaphysicians to the metaphysicians to produce some tangible result, some physical proof, that it offers practical utility and aid to humanity. The metaphysical response to this challenge has been fairly predictable. They believe that they are being forced into a cul-de-sac, a no-win situation where abstract reflection and subjective treatment are dismissed as unworthy if they do not immediately generate any scientific evidence to prove their validity or justify their existence. In other words, the metaphysicians refuse to accept an antimetaphysical disputation that attempts to "define" metaphysics out of existence. Such a definition is not acceptable to metaphysicians, and they claim that it is fallacious to assert that every reputable branch of knowledge must possess obvious, tangible, and easily applicable decision procedures or results. They illustrate their point by comparing metaphysics to the field of history.

Metaphysicians claim that there are innumerable areas of historical study where disputes, disagreements, and a noticeable lack of tangible proof play a major role. Yet each side of the dispute claims to, and indeed succeeds in the claim of proffering understanding and enlightenment. "Once we pass beyond the mere ascertaining of fact, there are many histories, written from many points of view, and resting on many judgements about what is historically valuable" (Walsh, 1967, p. 305). It is difficult to decide the merits of these differing historically sophisticated interpretations. "However, we don't conclude from this that history is a pointless pursuit which rational men would do best to avoid" (Walsh, 1967, p. 305). Indeed, such pursuits, even in their disagreements, imperfections, and lack of tangible utility, continually enlarge the mind and educate the understanding. When there are failures of any kind within an historical context, the criticism is, as it should be, aimed at the failure of the historian, not at the entire field of history. Metaphysicians claim that true utility is not entirely based on totally objective, pragmatic constraints. Utility is just as much a product of higher principles as it is of a spur of the moment pragmatism. This belief that higher principles are at least as important in determining utility as objective quantification usually leads metaphysicians into an investigation of certain absolutes from which their higher principles are derived. The question of utility invariably leads to this investigation of absolute principles because when one discusses utility, the usefulness of one thing as compared to another, one is actually making a judgment about what is real and what is good.

Any philosophical system accepts certain concepts as truth and abandons other concepts as being untrue. The reason for the acceptance of some ideas and the rejection of others is the belief that such acceptance or rejection can be translated into an individual or communal "good." Some decision is made about what is real and what is good. Every philosophical system either implicitly or explicitly makes such a decision and then carries this decision one step further by declaring that whatever is seen as real and good is also useful. It has utilitarian application in areas of thought and action. All philosophical systems make use of this relationship between the real, the good, and the useful. For purposes of example, the ideas of Idealism reveal this connection. An individual member of a society not aspiring to the common good is often sloughed off into the abyss of nonexistence along with ideas not relating to the communal good. Such individuals and such ideas are not useful because they are not good for the society and are therefore considered nonexistent (Butler, 1951). In primitive societies, this nonexistence is very literal, and individuals who are not good for the society are also not useful to it and are permanently (death) removed from said society. Such a primitive society serves as an excellent illustration of the relationship between the real, the good, and the useful. There is very little argument over such a relationship, but there is a great deal of dispute over the idea of who decides what is real and what is good and, consequently, useful, and also over the question of how this decision is reached.

These judgments about reality and goodness represent the heart of the problem. When antimetaphysicians adopt a reality and a system of value that includes only the objective, verifiable, and quantifiable realm of sensory translated phenomena and behavior, it closes off all appeal to a subjective nature of man. This appears to beg the question and again dismisses metaphysics by the simple act of "defining" it out of existence. This works only if everyone accepts such definitions, and metaphysicians refuse to accept this premise. Every theory and every practice logically follows from however followers of different positions answer this question, "What is real and what is good?" When metaphysics accepts a subjective nature for man in its consideration of reality and goodness, it marks a fundamental break between itself and antimetaphysics. The manner in which these qualities of ultimacy are dealt with is of tremendous importance because these answers will be reflected in every utilitarian and practical decision of each position. The basic positions taken toward reality and goodness are essentially relativistic (antimetaphysical) and absolutist (metaphysical).

The willingness of metaphysicians to deal in words such as absolute, ultimate, and other kindred terms has always been called into question by more relativistic thinkers. In his work entitled "Defense of Common Sense," G. E. Moore (1925) leveled many criticisms at metaphysics for delving into questions of absolutes with not only very little success, but also with very little need, since he contended that the world could be more adequately described in relative terms without resorting to esoteric arguments about the absolute nature of things. Ludwig Wittgenstein (1922) also addressed the relative versus absolute question. He labeled the entire notion of any ultimate description of the world a very suspect premise. David Hume's (1912) criticisms are even more blunt. He stated that there are no universals except those in the language we use to describe the world. These scholars contend that some philosophers confuse the fact that it is only a linguistic convenience to give the same name to resembling objects. Dewey (1916) succinctly echoed this theme when he stated that reality is not universal. It is simply what has been agreed upon by a particular community of inquirers. It is not unchangeable but is relative to perception in any given unit of experience. Labels are employed, but as Wittgenstein (1922) stated this is done out of linguistic convenience, not because of some single, absolute, universal principle tying independent particulars together.

Wittgenstein (1922) stressed that there are no ultimate truths and no absolute realities, and it has been philosophy's principal folly to cling to the idea that the primary function of language is to reach ultimate descriptions. "The truth is, rather, that we engage in many different language 'games,' each of which serves its own purpose and each of which is authentic at its own level" (Walsh, 1967, p. 305). Accordingly, no such game should be ruled out. To Wittgenstein (cited in Walsh, 1967), the fact that the game is played is sufficient evidence of its appropriateness and value. Also it seems to be Wittgenstein's (1922) belief that different sets of language users are not rivals in any sense of the word. One set of language users is just as authentic as any other set. The major point the antimetaphysicians seem to be raising is the vain attempt by metaphysics to unify all language games into an idea of a finally correct language which embraces all other language games. Wittgenstein (1922) stated that the key issue is not the idea of unification or absolute principles, but rather the notion of keeping all the diverse languages apart. In this way, it can clearly be seen that each has its own point to make, its own utility, and its own relative truth.

Philosophers with opposing views say that Wittgenstein's analysis is built on questionable assumptions (Hocutt, 1980). They claim that the so-called language games and all other areas of linguistic activity are not as distinct as Wittgenstein portrays them. For instance, in the language game of science and the games of common sense, most scientists and many plain men afford a higher priority to the so-called "expert" viewpoint. This expert is apt to play a more authentic game than the common sense users (Walsh, 1967). In other words, a more valid picture of the physical world is usually embodied in the scientific account than in the ordinary man's everyday beliefs. This fact calls into question Wittgenstein's contention that one language game is just as authentic as any other. There is also the possibility that Wittgenstein's belief that a language game is authentic simply because it is played is a highly questionable thesis. "After all, there are games, and then there are Games" (Walsh, 1967, p. 306).

An illustration can be found when one looks at the form of a game much played in the ancient world. In this game, elaborate formulas to appease the god of the sea were devised by those about to embark on a sea journey. As a result, a certain language game came into wide use and acceptability. But metaphysicians question Wittgenstein's belief that this alone can be invoked to illustrate legitimacy.

> Surely one would want to object that however much such language was used, its use could not be legitimate if in fact there were no god of the sea or if he exercised no influence on whether seafarers reached their destination safely. (Walsh, 1967, p. 306)

In raising this objection, metaphysicians are saying that the propriety of a language is subject to the tenability of the factual assumptions on which it rests. This does not mean that the only use of language is to describe, but they insist that it does lay a claim for certain priorities to be established in language games. Some games are simply worth more than others. The games that are worth more than others must be those

> which affect, or might affect, every man. Though these affections are necessarily as various as are individual conditions, yet the method must be such that the conclusion of every man shall be the same [universality] or would be the same if inquiry were sufficiently persisted in... There are real things, whose characters are entirely independent of our opinions about them; those realities affect our senses according to regular laws, and, though sensations are as different as our relations to the objects, yet, by taking advantage of the laws of perception, we can ascertain by reasoning how things really are, and any man,

> if he have sufficient experience and reason enough about it, will be led to the one true conclusion. (Peirce, 1966, pp. 107–108)

Metaphysicians claim that its concern is to attempt to identify those language games with one true conclusion. This constitutes the highest priority. It "is concerned with resolving conflicts by finding a way of speaking which will enable us to express the ultimate reality of the world" (Walsh, 1967, p. 306). If such language games are identified, one could derive a yardstick to measure the ultimate tenability, as opposed to immediate or relative use, of particular language games, such as the language game of religion, science, or law. Even though these particular games are constantly used and understood and obviously serve a purpose, this does not make it self-evident that they are truly authentic in any ultimate sense. Nor does it show that they are suited for the purpose which those who use them have in mind. "These games are indeed played, but they could, for all that, be played on false pretenses" (Walsh, 1967, p. 306). Metaphysicians feel that the only way to examine these games to discover their purpose or their authenticity is through metaphysical inquiry.

In any discussion of the absolute or ultimate quality of authenticity, the word truth usually finds its way into the debate. In fact, the absolute-relative argument is centered on the concept of truth. In his book *First Philosophy*, Max Hocutt (1980) examined the question of absolute versus relative truth. He stated that in today's world the popular theory seems to be that there is no such thing as *the* truth. Instead, there are opinions, each true for the person having that particular opinion, but none of the opinions true in any absolute sense. A simple analogy can be constructed to refute such a theory. One can say that the earth is flat to those who choose to believe it so, but that in no way proves that truth is relative to opinion. All that is stated in such a position is that some people believe the world to be flat. It asserts nothing about the shape of the earth, only about someone's opinion of that shape. The truth is that the earth is round whatever one may believe of it (Hocutt, 1980). It is utterly absurd to argue as William James (cited in Hocutt, 1980) did, that since the people of ancient times thought the earth was flat and now we think it round, the truth about the earth's shape changed. The point to be made here is the idea that the shape of the earth, as is the case in everything else, is not subject to opinion. Since the issue being discussed is the metaphysical position about absolute truth and not about the earth's shape, one could be expansive in this discussion and give in to the demands of the "flatearthers" and declare the earth to indeed be flat. But this changes nothing about the idea of the absolute quality of truth. Either statement can be right and be an example of absolute truth, but both statements (the earth is round/the earth is flat) cannot be true as the relativists and antimetaphysicians claim. Being magnanimous and saying that everyone has a right to one's own opinion is not the same as saying that everyone's opinion is right. "Opinions are relative, truth is absolute" (Hocutt, 1980, p. 35).

Other metaphysicians have also looked into this question and believe that they have proposed several logical conundrums for those holding the relativist position. The relativists have two major contentions. The first is the statement that all claims to truth are false claims (Drennen, 1962). If this statement is false, then there is no problem, because if it is false it means that there is truth and the stated position has no validity. If the statement is true, then it claims to be true on the basis of denying truth. This then is at least one truth, even though its apparent content is a denial of truth. "It is no use to admit that this would constitute an exception to prove its own rule, because a single lapse of a universal statement is as good as a total lapse" (Drennen, 1962, p. 150). Drennen (1962) presented a second relativist argument which says that "one cannot be sure of anything" (p. 150). Metaphysicians point out that this statement must itself take its place as a member of the "anything" class. This of course means that the statement is as uncertain as everything else, which in turn means that it is worthless as a proposition. The implication, though, is that one thing is certain, namely this statement. The statement, however, claims total uncertainty. The contradictions are considered so obvious that metaphysicians consider further examination of the relativist position to be spurious.

There are, of course, other specific antimetaphysical positions that can serve as examples of questionable propositions. Carnap (1959) stated that truth is relative to the process of experimentation. A complete definition (affirmation or denial) is available on the relative merits of each experiment. Another brief example of the "spurious" nature of the antimetaphysical position being examined is the idea of William James' "Neutral Stuff," where precepts, including truth, are neither mental nor physical; rather they are neutral and depend entirely on the relative circumstances of a particular problem in a particular point in time (Krikorian & Edel, 1959). These examples represent a brief sampling of the arguments that metaphysicians find questionable. Many of these points will be dealt with in more detail at a later time.

The late Robert Maynard Hutchins (1943), a lifelong spokesman for the metaphysical position, deeply lamented the rise in the general acceptance of the antimetaphysical position of relativism. He wrote

(1943) that many members of modern society believe that if anyone outside of a natural science says he knows anything, he should be branded a dogmatist and an authoritarian. Those who take no stand on any issue because "all things are relative" are seen as liberal, progressive, democratic fellows to whom the fate of the world may be safely entrusted.

The line separating the absolutists and relativists is the belief that such absolutes as truth exist, and the belief that it would be a most beneficial and legitimate effort to inquire into the nature of these ultimate concerns. Metaphysicians continue to research the idea that there are certain concrete standards (absolutes) which exist regardless of our inability to attain perceptual or objective knowledge of them. This inability to attain perceptual, objective knowledge and the unwillingness to accept the objective knowledge generated by natural science as the final authority is the demarcation line separating modern metaphysicians and antimetaphysicians. The question of perceptual and nonperceptual knowledge is a restatement of the ancient question, what is it, and how is it that we can know? The philosophical movement known as logical positivism is a perfect example of the antimetaphysical position on this key question of what and how can we know.

Positivism is used as an example of this issue for two major reasons: first, because the positivists are so precise in explaining how they believe the process of knowing takes place and they, perhaps more than any other movement, lend clarity to the antimetaphysical stance on this issue; second, the positivistic movement is one of the key sources incorporated in the learning theory and knowledge theory of environmental psychology.

The positivists say that one can know only what the physical senses can reveal, and also that the only knowledge that is acceptable is that which can be verified through sensory processes (that which can be physically observed) (Ayer, 1945). Metaphysicians claim that there is more to ultimate reality and knowledge than sense perception alone can decipher. This question of the importance of verifiability marks the rise of the logical positivists as the standard-bearer of antimetaphysics, and although the philosophy of the logical positivists has been largely discredited in philosophy, it remains a powerful force in psychology.

The beginnings of modern positivism can be found in the works of David Hume and John Locke and have progressed through the works of Bertrand Russell, A. J. Ayer, Rudolph Carnap, Morris Lazerowitz, and other disciples of the movement. It should be noted that positivism basically subscribes to the preceding antimetaphysical arguments dealt with so far in this book, but its major belief is the idea that experimental science and observational verification form the basis of all knowledge worth the name and all of reality that can be known. Since the subjectivity of metaphysics fails to conform to the strict observational guidelines of experimental science, it is said not to add to the sum of human knowledge or understanding. To those espousing this view, metaphysics is a sham. Positivists have, with much vitriol and vituperance, pointed out the experiential failings of all subjective modes of thought. In *The Structure of Metaphysics*, Morris Lazerowitz (1955) said that, though metaphysical problems are intrinsically insoluble, they are believable to a point, just as a psychotic's dream is believable to a psychiatrist. The only difference between the psychotic and the metaphysician is one is institutionalized while the other is allowed to run free. In *Language, Truth, and Logic*, A. J. Ayer (1945) stated that transcendent or a priori knowledge of any kind is at best spurious and at worst a hoax. All so-called metaphysical utterances are said to be due either to the commission of logical errors, linguistic errors, or nonsensical errors. The positivists propose the idea that all that can truly be said to constitute genuine propositions are tautologies and empirical hypotheses. When any stated proposition fails to meet the criterion of empirical verification, it ceases to be a genuine proposition. Metaphysical and subjective propositions fail to be empirically verifiable; therefore it follows that such statements are nonsensical. The totality of this positivistic pronouncement is seen in the belief that "the only method of attaining knowledge is the method used in the natural sciences, and hence, no kind of knowledge is genuine unless it is natural science or resembles natural science in method" (Collingwood, 1940, p. 143). "The claims of traditional philosophers, alchemists, astrologers, or magicians are now rejected...because their results are not testable, reliable, and coherent with the rest of public knowledge" (Soltis, 1978, p. 8). In a similar spirit, Hume (cited in Drennen, 1962) said that metaphysics could be considered as either poetry or nonsense but not as knowledgeable propositions. Any metaphysics containing neither analysis nor experimental reasonings should be destroyed, "for it can contain nothing but sophistry and illusion" (p. 149). Positivism contends that the world is totally sensory in nature and as such it can only be interpreted or perceived through sensory experience. This cornerstone of positivism is made quite clear in the words of John Locke (cited in Yolton, 1967): "Experience is the source of our knowledge of a world of object or phenomena" (p. 49). Hume (cited in Yolton, 1980) echoed this premise when he said that "conception [ideas, thoughts, etc.] cannot go beyond experience" (p. 9).

The positivists' key for deciding what could truly pass for knowledge is the so-called principle of verifiability. Ayer (1945) defined this principle by stating that literal significance and verifiability can only occur when certain observational conditions are met, so as to lead one to accept or reject a proposition. The key word here is observational. The principle of verifiability belongs solely to the domain of science and the scientific method. Lazerowitz (1955) said that when metaphysics is held up to the light of scientific inquiry and observational verifiability it shows its true value.

> We see the worthlessness of metaphysics when we contrast it with the special sciences, with their imposing edifices of sound results, while metaphysics is in a chronic condition of endless and unresolved debate (p. 157).

Carnap (1953) added that there can be only two kinds of questions in a scientific enterprise of any literal significance. There are object-questions, which are concerned with concrete objects of a specific domain, and logical-questions which are concerned only with the referents of concrete objects. Since, to Carnap, metaphysics deals only with suppositious objects not to be found in the concrete object domain of science, it can only ask pseudoquestions. These pseudoquestions cannot be answered because its object cannot show up in empirical science. This leaves metaphysics in a tangled mess and only by disentangling itself will it have value, and yet when metaphysics is untangled (purified of all unscientific and non-observable elements) only the logic of science remains. (Carnap, 1953, pp. 278–279). This total faith in sensory experience stands as a cardinal assumption in the positivistic movement.

Another basic principle is the belief that thinking is a process whereby facts are ascertained through the senses and then arranged in an orderly fashion with concepts merely being seen as a class of facts. Since facts are, by definition of the positivists, observable (where to observe means to ascertain by the use of the senses), a concept is valid only if the facts of which it is a class are observable facts, which they could be known to be only on condition that they are observed. Stated simply, this is nothing more than a process of observing facts in order to understand experience or, as Ayer (1945) put it, no legitimate proposition can exist without sensory verification. Metaphysicians claim that sensate material plays a part in conceptualizing, but positivism seems to state that it is the conceptual process itself. Lazerowitz (1955) claimed that, by referring to absolute truth and other terms of "deep meanings," metaphysicians are making things unnecessarily difficult because of a selfish ulterior motive. By being so esoteric, they justify their existence as speculators about the "reasons behind things" and by convincing others that such deep meanings exist and that it is the task of metaphysics to uncover such meanings, they are simply attempting to make themselves indispensable. Through references to deeper meanings, metaphysicians are hoping that, through complex linguistic games, they can make things so difficult to understand that no one would notice the bankrupt and confusing nature of their philosophical assets. The positivists believe that they have revealed this intellectual bankruptcy by stripping away the unnecessary complexity of metaphysical erudition and proclaiming that all knowledge comes through sensory experience and is empirically verifiable through the modern scientific method.

To the positivist, philosophy is not an instrument for discovering that which is true or false, or that which is real or merely apparent. Rather, philosophy's task is only to clarify the meanings of statements. When these statements are clarified, some will be shown to be scientific, some to be mathematical, and some to be nonsensical. The first two of these categories are statements of literal significance. The nonsensical statements have no literal significance. Positivists state that the pronouncements of metaphysics belong to the nonsense category. Such statements are not about the real world, and they are not empirically verifiable and are therefore nonsense (Ayer, 1945). The positivists refer to statements of literal significance as synthetic statements. "Synthetic statements are informative by nature of their empirical verification" (Popkin & Stroll, 1956, p. 183). Thus, to the positivist, a statement of genuine knowledge does not come from a process of abstract, subjective conceptual thinking because such modes of thought cannot be verified. Genuine knowledge comes only if one knows what observations would lead one, under certain conditions, to accept a proposition as true or false (Ayer, 1945).

In summary, it can be said that the antimetaphysical thrust of positivism embraces four major thoughts at its foundation: (a) the belief that the method of natural science is the only valid road to knowledge; (b) the belief that all knowledge is sensory in nature; (c) the belief that all "true" knowledge is verifiable through observation; and (d) the belief that philosophy's task is to engender linguistic clarity and not to delve into abstract speculations about ultimate reality or to engage in any prescriptory behavior concerning right or wrong.

The aforementioned arguments for positivism of course represent only one side of the philosophic coin. Modern metaphysicians take issue with virtually every plank in the positivist platform. Etiene Gilson (1937) observed that a study of the history of philosophy reveals that there have always been perceptible periods of belief and disbelief regarding metaphysics. In every instance history shows that disbelief has always been followed by belief, and metaphysics has always gained more than it lost in defending itself. Certainly, it cannot be said that metaphysics has suffered any mortal wounds from its skeptics. The simple fact is that metaphysics makes a habit of burying its undertakers (Gilson, 1937). So, to Gilson at least, metaphysics shows its worth historically by being able to survive and flourish while many of its detractors have disappeared. The implication is that the same fate awaits positivism.

Frederick C. Copleston in *A Realistic Rejoinder* (ed. Drennen, 1962) has perhaps more adequately pursued the historical impact of metaphysics. He noted that the positivist movement sees metaphysics as nothing more than linguistic satire or as pseudosolutions to pseudoproblems, with both the solution and the problem being meaningless. "But metaphysical questions cannot be dismissed out of hand unless they are first formulated" (p. 164). If meaningful questions can also be shown to be metaphysical questions, it provides a key counter-argument against positivism. Copleston (ed. Drennen, 1962) argued that this can be done using positivism's own linguistic analysis. When one describes material objects, such as tables, in terms of "logical constructs," a metaphysical theory is being posed.

> To say that statements about phenomena, a table for instance, are the equivalent of statements about sense data [as is asserted by the positivists] is to propose a metaphysical thesis since it is the result of a philosophical analysis of meaning. (Copleston, ed. Drennen, 1962, p. 163)

This is reminiscent of F. H. Bradley's contention that the so-called antimetaphysicians are nonexistent, that they are simply brother metaphysicians posing a rival metaphysical theory. Copleston (ed. Drennen, 1962) argued that statements about phenomena and its empirical existence cannot be made without a primary implicit awareness of its existence against a background of being. The implicit background of being precedes the explicit foreground of empirical existence. To debate this point is the same as saying that an answer can come before its own question. Collingwood (1940) noted that "a question is logically prior to its own answer" (p. 63). A thing has to "be" before it can be measured empirically. If this assertion is not accepted, then one must prove oneself able to measure something that does not exist. This obviously cannot be done.

Copleston is certainly not the only one to point out problems in the positivist position regarding phenomena (the belief that knowledge is strictly limited to the appearance of things and not the things themselves). A. E. Taylor (1903) also argued against the contention that appearances (called phenomena) are all that can be known, and also against the belief that what lies behind phenomena is completely inaccessible, thus making speculation about the nature of that which underlies appearances a total waste of time. The positivist procedure is to use the senses alone to discover the general laws and uniformities of the interconnections of phenomena and simply dismiss the problem of the background of being as insoluble. Metaphysicians state that such a procedure is a classic example of oversimplification. Taylor (1903) pointed out that those who support this positivist line of thought make so many contradictory statements that, in the end, their position borders on the incredible. First, those opposed to abstract reasoning state that nothing can be known about ultimate reality, but they contradictorily assert "that it is a certain and ultimate truth that all phenomena are connected by general laws, and that the course of nature is, without exception, uniform" (p. 11). Taylor revealed a flaw in the positivist position when he pointed out that the positivists state that ultimate reality is unknowable and then contradictorily use this principle to defend their own cardinal assumptions and thus create an indefensible position. He sees an even greater contradiction in the positivist dictum that "we know only phenomena" (Taylor, 1903, p. 11). He stated that "this statement is meaningless unless enough is known about ultimate realities to be sure that they are unknowable" (p. 11). His point is that those espousing the position that ultimate reality is unknowable "commit themselves to the recognition of at least one proposition as an absolute or ultimate truth, namely the proposition that, 'I know that whatever I know is mere appearance'" (p. 11). In *The Unity of Philosophical Experience*, Gilson (1937) argued that, by claiming that all knowledge comes from sensory experience, one asserts that the statement itself (all knowledge comes from sensory experience) comes from sensory experience also. Obviously this cannot be. Leibnitz (cited in Gilson, 1937) said that there is nothing in the intellect that has not first been in sense, except the intellect itself. Gilson (1937) further argued that the typical attributes of scientific knowledge, universality and necessity, are not found in sensible reality. He (1937) noted also that, though Kant may have been one of the first to really distrust metaphysical speculation, he early recognized that there is more in rational knowledge than one finds in sensory experience. Kant's ideas about the irreversibility of time and the fact that no two objects can occupy the same space at the same time are illustrative of the point. Neither of these two ideas can be accounted for through sensory experience. Both are simply concepts of the mind. The fact that they are not observable is clear, but it is also clear that these concepts do exist as knowledge regardless of the fact that they are unaccounted for sensationally.

Such examples as these seem to uphold the assertion that there are concepts which exist in the mind only and not in experience and yet these mental concepts are still considered knowledge. This reinforces the metaphysical belief that there are indeed questions and propositions that are not sensory in nature but are still meaningful. Many philosophers feel that this contention calls into question the basic positivist premise, the principle of verifiability. As previously stated, this principle holds that any meaningful question or proposition is derived purely through the senses because this is the only way the statements can be empirically verified, and only empirically verifiable statements can be true. Metaphysicians use this definition to make another point for their position. Drennen (1962) claimed that, by subjecting the statement (only empirical statements are true) to its own logic, a basic flaw presents itself. The statement is self-referable. Therefore, the question can be asked, on what empirical grounds is this statement itself advanced? Is it or is it not, itself, empirical? Reason dictates that if it is not empirical then the statement is self-destructive. If it is claimed to be empirical, then it must be shown *how* it is empirically verifiable. This is not demonstrable. The statement that only empirical statements are true is not equivalent to the proposition that empirical sentences can be verified and therefore are true statements. These statements are different because "the original statement, though applicable to a 'laboratory' proposition, is not itself a 'laboratory' proposition, it is only a universalized statement about such propositions" (Drennen, 1962, pp. 150–151). One simply cannot pretend that verifying particular instances of a generalization is the same as verifying the generalization itself. To those supporting the position of metaphysics, this once again illustrates the point that there are meaningful statements which are neither tautologies nor empirical constructs.

In attempting to show that meaning and ultimate reality can transcend tautological and empirical confines, A. E. Taylor (1903) in the book *Elements of Metaphysics* attempted to establish the counterarguments needed to blunt the criticisms of the positivists. He stated that, by dealing with only phenomena and appearance and ignoring that which lies behind appearance, those who oppose metaphysics are ignoring a fundamental question. If there is no rational foundation for the distinction between reality and appearance, then all science is a total illusion. If there is any meaning in the distinction between the real and the apparent, then it is clearly a necessary and proper question to ask what those distinctions might be (Taylor, 1903). The right to ask such questions can only be opposed by one who is prepared to maintain that "the contradictions which lead one to make the distinctions may themselves be the ultimate truth about things" (Taylor, 1903, pp. 8–9). This argument is itself a metaphysical theory of first principles and it has to be defended, if it can be defended at all, by an elaborate metaphysical analysis of the meaning of "truth" and "reality." This poses a denial of metaphysics which can only be advanced through the use of a metaphysical theory. The contradiction is evident. If such self-contradictory propositions can be true, "then there is no rational ground for preferring a coherent scientific theory of the world to the wildest dreams of superstition or insanity" (Taylor, 1903, p. 9). The only way to avoid such self-contradictory dilemmas is to acknowledge that there are rational foundations for the distinctions between reality and appearance. If such acknowledgements are made, then "we are logically bound to inquire into the principles of the distinctions" (Taylor, 1903, p. 9), thereby facing the problems of metaphysics.

Taylor (1903) also called into question the positivistic idea that all intelligible questions about reality fall within the provinces of one of the "pure sciences." This constitutes the contention that there can be no facts with which some one or other of the sciences do not deal. The key point to such a contention is that it leaves no room for metaphysical inquiry over and above scientific inquiry. "When there are facts to investigate and intelligible questions to answer, we are in the domain of science, and when there are no such facts or questions, there can be no knowledge" (Taylor, 1903, p. 9). This argument is based on "a flagrant fallacy of 'Petitio principii'" (Taylor, 1903, p. 9). It makes the groundless assumption that there is no science in the most universal acceptance of the term (no body of reasoned truth) beside those experimental sciences which have for their object the accumulation and systematization of facts. Those espousing such a position do so because they do not understand the intent of metaphysical analysis. Metaphysics does not assert that there is a body of facts with which the various special branches of experimental science cannot deal. Metaphysics only asserts that there are questions which ought to be raised about the facts with which these sciences deal (Taylor, 1903). These are questions which experimental inquiry is incapable of addressing. This idea is echoed quite frequently in the works of the noted American educator, Robert Maynard Hutchins. In *Education for Freedom*, Hutchins (1943) stated that metaphysics is not a competitor of science, nor is it trying to replace science. Science must be used to answer many questions, but one uses science to get to a destination. Science is a device to travel there, but it is not the destination itself. It can give directions to goals, but it is not itself the goal.

> Science can be employed for good or evil purposes, but men have the purposes and they do not learn them from science... From a scientific investigation one can expect scientific knowledge and nothing more. (Hutchins, 1943, p. 34)

Those who call for the dissolution of metaphysics on the grounds that all worthwhile knowledge is a result of experimental science place themselves in an indefensible position. This position can be vouchsafed only if it can be shown that experimental science is infallible and this cannot be done. There are numerous examples in the annals of experimental science that show the fallibility of the experimenter, the experimental design, or the concept undergirding the experiment. Since this present study is most interested in the relationship between environmental and humanistic psychology and philosophy, perhaps an example of the fallibility of experimental science in the area of psychology would best serve the point being made here. Collingwood (1940) cited certain errors made by psychology even though it purported to use the experimental method. In Professor C. Spearman's book *The Nature of Intelligence and the Principles of Cognition* (1923), the author stated several psychological "laws" which he claimed to have established through minute and highly scientific experiments. On page 132 of this text, Spearman provided "the principle of retentivity: the occurrence of any cognitive event produces a tendency for it to occur after" (Spearman, cited in Collingwood, 1940, p. 126). On page 134 Spearman states the "principle of fatigue: the occurrence of any cognitive event produces a tendency opposed to it occurring afterward" (Spearman, cited in Collingwood, 1940, p. 126). Collingwood (1940) stated that regardless of the experimental nature of these "laws," they are contradictory and are of no value to anyone. Again using Professor Spearman's book, Collingwood quotes from pages 229–230:

> Thus, then, the mental event asserted, more speculatively than evidentially by a long array of writers—Plato [through] the "impressions" of Hume and most associationists—receives finally an experimental corroboration. (Spearman, cited in Collingwood, 1940, p. 128)

Collingwood again called the author to account because he claimed to have discovered something by the methods of experimental science that others had been saying speculatively for well over 2,000 years. The difference is that he asserts it evidentially, while others asserted it only speculatively. The only point to this experimental exercise is to say that when Plato guessed, he guessed right. If this is the case,

> Professor Spearman's researches are useless. If they had [proved] Plato's guess wrong, they would have at least done something, but for the preceding 2,000 years and more every one had believed Plato's guess to be right, and as the Professor allows us to do that still, his researches have left the subject exactly where he found it. (Collingwood, 1940, p. 129).

Because of these and other similar examples, metaphysicians totally reject the notion that metaphysics is useless because science and practical experience already supply a coherent theory of the world, devoid of error and contradiction.

The best representatives of mathematical and experimental science seem absolutely agreed that ultimate questions about first principles are outside the scope of their science. Every science is defined by certain initial assumptions. This statement does not come simply from metaphysical thinkers. Rather, this is an implicit rule adopted by the scientists themselves. They acknowledge the fact that great contradictions and errors are committed when a science makes exaggerated claims that lie beyond the initial assumptions of that science. What does not fall within a science's assumptions must be treated as nonexistent (Taylor, 903). For instance, if the mathematician follows the initial assumptions of the field, he/she is restricted to dealing with problems of number and quantity. Whether or not "there are realities which are in their own nature non-numerical and non-quantitative, the mathematician is not called upon to pronounce" (Taylor, 1903, p. 12). If there are such realities (and the science does not assert the contrary) then that science, by its initial assumptions, prevents one from knowing anything about them. Thus, the metaphysicians claim that the sciences should only deal with those questions which fall within the sphere of their initial assumptions.

As is often the case though, one science's discoveries, within its initial assumptions, will go in the opposite direction of the discoveries of another science. Also, one can easily envision questions which arise when science points in one direction and deep religious or ethical experiences point in an opposite direction. Questions of this type are not covered in the initial assumptions of the various experimental sciences. Metaphysicians claim that questions of this nature lie beyond the scope of science and can only be dealt with metaphysically. This should not be taken to mean that metaphysics lays claim to some mystical body of knowledge known only to itself and lying outside the purview of science. Metaphysics deals "with the same facts which forms the province of the sciences, but it deals with those facts which form that province from a point of view which is not that of experimental science" (Taylor, 1903, p. 10). Rarely has the science versus metaphysics issue been propagated by noteworthy men of science. It is generally conceded that such a debate is out of their field (Taylor, 1903). It is Taylor's (1903) contention that metaphysics deals with issues in exactly the same manner as each of the individual sciences. Sciences do not deal with different sets of facts. They deal with the same facts but from a different point of view.

> Thus physics, physiology, and psychology deal with the same set of facts...an involuntary movement...and examine it from different perspectives: physics as a series of displacements of mass particles, physiology as a combination of muscular contractions initiated from a center in the cortex of the brain, psychology as a step to the satisfaction of a felt want. (Taylor, 1903, p. 10)

Examining a set of facts from a metaphysical viewpoint often means a certain "sameness" in metaphysical speculation. This has resulted in the antimetaphysical claim that, since metaphysics continues to perpetuate the same problems, it should be abandoned. "Metaphysical problems are, in a sense, always the same, but this is equally true of the problems of any other science" (Taylor, 1903, p. 13). The methods and solutions may vary from age to age, but the basic problems remain the same.

This idea is opposed to the antimetaphysical doctrine of what Lazerowitz (1955) referred to as the sound edifices of methodology as compared to the useless abstractions of traditional philosophy. This idea of Lazerowitz implies that the antimetaphysicians are really doing something tangible while metaphysics is only disorganized abstract mental meanderings. But metaphysics has its methodological side and indeed there are those who contend that no methodology can exist without the ideas embodied in traditional philosophy.

> Classical positivists say that philosophy in the traditional sense is an organized body of pseudo-knowledge, but in any case, organized, and this is important. Some methodological regularities in this organization or articulation may be presupposed almost automatically. Then to study the features of this organization can be a proper task of a discipline which is concerned with methods, particularly with the methods used in philosophy. (Riska, 1972, p. 221)

> Methodological awareness started within the realm of philosophy...e.g., explicitly in Aristotle's *Organum* and later in Descarts... So the articulations of philosophical conceptions makes it possible for methodology to consider philosophy as a subject matter of investigation (the opposite also holds true), which in a static linguistic form reflects the stages of philosophical problems, to reach some goals by penetration, say into the essence of the world, man, value, knowledge, and similar concepts, domains, or entities. Only a view that philosophy in its linguistic or conceptual expression is totally disorganized, or at least disorganized to such an extent that it remains in a stage of methodological immaturity could refute the methodological status of philosophy. (Since refutation on these grounds is not possible) philosophers form and express their conceptions and do not follow the "silencing" maximum of Wittgenstein. (Riska, 1972, p. 222)

This is as it should be, since metaphysics is intimately intertwined with scientific method. A careful reading of history confirms the idea that metaphysics and science have never been antagonists, but rather have been interdependent partners. "Every great metaphysical conception exerts a general influence on science and in return every great movement in science affects metaphysical inquiry" (Taylor, 1903, p. 13).

Thus a revived interest in 17th century mechanical science affected the metaphysical method and result of Descarts. The advent of the Calculus and also Leuwenhoeck's discoveries in embryology greatly influenced Leibnitz. Even today there is much evidence of the symbiotic liaison between science and metaphysics. Much present metaphysical speculation revolves around the scientific ideas concerning the conservation of energy and the origin of species by gradual differentiation. Each fundamental scientific discovery demands a restatement and a reconsideration of an old metaphysical problem in light of the new scientific discovery. The major questions may remain the same, but the consideration of these questions is markedly influenced by science and tends to great diversity. Thus, "metaphysics is stagnant only if one considers that all science is stagnant" (Taylor, 1903, p.13).

The preceding outline of the fundamental metaphysical position reveals the basic antagonism between antimetaphysics and metaphysics. In summation, it could be said that metaphysicians are opposed to every element of the antimetaphysical philosophic stance. They do not agree that the methods of natural science are the *only* way to knowledge. They contend that subjective methods cannot be dismissed as a potential path. Metaphysicians also make the claim that knowledge is more than sense perception (again taking an oppositional stance toward the antimetaphysicians) and can exist regardless of observational quantification or verifiability. Finally, they state that the major thrust of metaphysics must be directed toward the investigation of absolute and ultimate realities. They admit that the idea of linguistic clarity (espoused by the antimetaphysicians as a major thrust of philosophy) is beneficial in achieving the goal (attaining a proper intellectual attitude toward the ultimate reality) but they are strongly opposed to the idea that linguistic clarity is *the* goal. Chapter II expands on this antagonism between metaphysics and antimetaphysics by investigating the effect that this philosophic conflict has on modern counseling. Understanding the fundamental differences in metaphysics and antimetaphysics will help counselors to understand the modern counseling differences that have, in large degree, been engendered by the centuries old philosophic conflict.

There are many specialized counseling theories because in the normal process of theoretical adoption each counselor will choose a general theory to support and then will adapt that theory, with major or minor modifications, into a set of principles true to the counselor's own beliefs. In most cases, at the level of philosophical assumptions, the basic principles of these individual theories will be similar, but to prove this by trying to match each person's particular theory to a set of philosophical assumptions is a task ad infinitum and lies well beyond the aspirations of this book. A further generalization of counseling theory would be possible if one were to investigate the philosophical assumptions underlying the most widely accepted counseling theories. This is more feasible than an investigation of specific counselors' theories, but it would still be a monumental undertaking. One would have to investigate the philosophical assumptions of psychoanalysis, behaviorism, combinations of psychoanalysis and behaviorism (such as Miller and Dollard's work), trait-factor approaches, rational emotive therapy, Christian and agnostic versions of existentialism, gestalt, phenomenology, cognitive theories and others. Although such investigations are needed, again this is beyond the scope of this endeavor. In generalizing counseling to its most fundamental levels, one finds that there is something of a consensus that basically four major viable forces are present in modern counseling theory: the psychoanalytical or Freudian force, the environmentalist (subsuming all behavioral theories) force, the cognitive force, and the humanist force. It is at this level of generalization that this work will concern itself.

Psychoanalytic theory will not be discussed for two reasons: (a) The vast majority of modern counseling's concerns, in its literature, its training procedures, and its methodological supports, deal with environmental and humanist perspectives. Presently the Freudian force is the least dominant of the four main forces in counseling. This is not at all meant to belittle its contribution, but in the ebb and flow of theoretical domination, at this time, psychoanalysis is the least prominent of the four. This is, of course, subject to change with each new generation of counselors. (b) For purposes of clarity (since studies of a philosophical nature are somewhat uncommon in the field of counseling) this study focuses on the most widely divergent counseling movements (the cognitive force, often using both humanistic and environmental approaches, is something of a "compromise" approach and will not be dealt with in this book because it often lacks clear points of philosophical delineation). This divergence in counseling has previously been noted as far back as its relationship to the metaphysics-antimetaphysics positions. On most issues the positions exist as absolute polarities. Since a major tool of this study is comparative analysis, choosing theories that are widely opposed to one another on most issues will provide more clarity for the reader. For example, if one were discussing the differences in the nature of color, one might choose red and green for purposes of illustration or comparison. To choose different shades of blue might only confound the issue rather than add clarity. Similarly, since psychoanalysis has more overlapping philosophical assumptions than the other two forces, its consideration may be more prone to confusion.

The fact that both counseling forces selected have been in existence as distinct movements for a considerable period of time and thus have generated a significant body of historical information is most helpful. Thanks to this body of historical documentation, it is easy to see, as other authors (Barclay, Butler, and Misiak) have seen, a somewhat tangential but nonetheless distinct similarity between environmentalism and the major philosophical movement of pragmatism, and also between humanism and the philosophical position known as idealism. There are differences, of course, but the similarities greatly increased the availability of information in terms of relating counseling movements to philosophical movements.

Chapters IV and V will consist of an investigation of a representative theorist's (from each counseling movement) writings to provide evidence showing that the theorist's general philosophical outlook, theory, method, and practice are directly traceable to the philosophical assumptions of each position. Since this level of philosophic assumptions is the most ignored aspect of counseling, it is hoped that by dealing in a framework of specific metaphysical topics (Being, for example) and showing how each representative theorist draws his theories, methods, and practices from these basic metaphysical topics, counselors will find renewed interest and understanding for their own theoretical choices, and also gain a better understanding of the relationship between philosophical assumptions, theory, and practice. This is a crucial point. The manner in which each representative theorist deals with basic metaphysical topics will determine the theory and practical methodology of that theorist. The examination of the writings of the theorists will hopefully reveal the important implications that basic philosophical assumptions have for theory and practice. For example, how the theorist responds to the metaphysical topic of "value" will form the basis of the methods used to help a client. If the question of value is answered by the theoretician in such a way as to denote that behavior is either lawful or unlawful, then it becomes the task of the therapist to "help" a client judge right and wrong, and also to help him choose the "right" behavior. If the question of value is answered by saying that behavior is neither lawful nor unlawful, it is simply learned, then the task of the therapist has nothing to do with right or wrong. This therapist simply teaches a new behavior. One that is neither right nor wrong, just new.

The decision as to which counseling theorist could best represent the two movements being considered was difficult. One could conceivably choose any major theorist from the ranks of these two counseling movements. This would represent a choice of two theorists out of a field numbering literally in the hundreds. The difficulty involved in such a choice is quite obvious. Because of this overwhelming difficulty, it should be noted that there is no assertion that the two theorists selected are "the best" representative theorists of each respective movement. In point of fact, any theorist chosen would draw considerable criticism. The two theorists selected for study can be counted as representative theorists but certainly not *the* representative theorist of each movement. The choice is made more difficult by the fact that each counseling movement represents a very loose collection of subgroups and different theories. Sometimes these subgroupings differ on almost every issue except those philosophical assumptions that form their basis. This is especially true of the humanistic movement. The key things that make humanism a distinct movement are its philosophical assumptions and its conviction that environmentalistic theories are not the proper direction for counseling to take. It is important to remember, though, that consistency in metaphysical structure is of much more consequence than differences in practice or methodology. Environmentalism has contradictions, of course, but its internal self-consistency makes it more clearly discernible as a distinct counseling movement. In some cases various humanistic theories differ, in terms of theory and practice, as much with other humanistic theories as with environmental positions. All of these points add together to insure from the outset that whichever theorists were chosen, the choices would neither please everyone nor be agreeable to everyone.

The choice of B. F. Skinner to represent environmentalism and Viktor Frankl to represent humanism was the result of several factors and influences. Skinner was chosen in spite of the fact that he is not a counseling theorist. He has no body of work detailing his specific counseling theories, methods, and practices. But despite this, Skinner's writings have been a most influential (some say *the* most influential) force on those who have developed counseling strategies based on environmental precepts. Skinner's works have exerted a tremendous shaping force on the environmental school of thought, and although he is not a counseling theorist himself, his work exists as something of a fundamental wellspring from which other environmental theorists have continually drawn.

Another reason for selecting Skinner is that his writings reflect the belief that he is as much a theoretician as a practitioner of environmentalism. He seems equally concerned with the *why* as with the *how*. The basic concern of this book is at the level of philosophical assumptions and the relation of these assumptions to counseling theory. Although a relationship between theoretical assumptions and theory also presupposes a relationship between theory and practice, it is not the primary concern here to investigate the area of counseling practice. This made the selection of Skinner a promising one because, likewise, most of his writings are concerned with theory as much as with practice. If a therapist had been selected whose only concern was technique, then his/her works would first have to be studied to isolate the major techniques. These techniques would then have to be traced back to the theory which spawned them and only then could an investigation be undertaken to examine these theories in the context of their fundamental assumptions. The fact that Skinner deals with theory as much (and possibly more) as with practice (at least in his writings) makes this study easier by removing a need to examine a great body of methodology in an ancillary fashion before moving on to theory, the primary area of concern.

Skinner was also selected because of the prolific nature of his writings. He has written a rather large body of information concerning environmental thought, thus making his ideas very accessible and easy to investigate. Related to this issue was the fact of Skinner's literary longevity. The ability to study his works over a long period of time allows an investigator to assess and study the continuity of his ideas, how they have changed and evolved and grown. Finally, Skinner has been chosen because of his stature in the psychological and counseling world. Even to his detractors, Skinner is a noted and well-respected spokesman for his position. Selecting such a credible representative theorist as Skinner will hopefully enhance the credibility of this study.

There are several logical reasons for Frankl's selection as the representative of humanism. Like Skinner, Viktor Frankl is not overly concerned with technique. As previously mentioned, dealing with representatives who have a great interest in theory as well as practice assures that the focal point of this study, theory and theoretical assumptions, stays in the foreground and does not become overly diluted with methodological concerns. This also has the additional benefit of allowing a simpler comparative study between the two theorists. Since one of their areas of major concern is the same (theory), it makes for more points of comparison and sharpens the comparative differences and similarities in their works.

Other reasons for choosing Frankl were very similar to the criteria used in Skinner's selection. Frankl has a substantial body of written material explaining and extolling his own brand of humanistic strategies. Also Frankl, again like Skinner, has achieved a certain longevity. His writings have been in existence long enough to allow a considerable body of work by other authors, who chose as their subject the analysis of Frankl's teaching. This analysis of self and analysis by others makes it much less difficult to research Frankl's major theoretical constructs. Frankl has also played a very substantial role in structuring the humanistic movement and because of this and also because of the respect accorded him throughout the field of counseling, it was felt that he would be a very credible representative of humanism.

Unlike Skinner, Frankl is definitely a counseling theorist. He has composed whole counseling strategies, in terms of both theory and practice. He is a well-respected educator of other counselors also. In spite of these qualities, it remains a fact that many others from the field of humanism would meet these criteria and be as good a choice as Frankl. The choice of Skinner was relatively easier because he is such a dominant figure in the more self-consistent area of environmentalism. Humanism lacks both this one, single dominating figure and the self-consistency in theory and technique. Overall, though, Frankl's stature in the counseling community makes him a most acceptable representative of humanism.

The limitations of a book of this type are readily apparent. In fact, the limitations inherent in investigations of this nature probably constitute a major reason for the paucity of philosophical examination within the field of counseling. One limitation comes from the fact that the two counseling movements under scrutiny are basically opposed to one another and, without meaning to, one often subjectively takes one side over the other. In large measure, this is due to the fact that their philosophical forebearers were and still are antagonistic forces and human nature causes one to support a particular side in almost any antagonistic battle. Both counseling movements attest to their own worth and make claims of superiority. For a counselor writing in this area, it becomes a very difficult task to maintain objectivity and not "choose sides." This is a limitation because even subconsciously an author's bias can exert a significant influence on studies of this type. Since there is no basis for proving with any sense of finality the superiority or inferiority of one position over another, it becomes a difficult task to "rein in" one's subjective bias. The attempt has been made, but it must be acknowledged that the effort has not always been successful.

Another limitation is common to any scientific enterprise. This limitation stems from the fact that before any method can be evaluated it first has to be used.

> The true character of any scientific method can only be discovered by the actual use of it; a preliminary disquisition on the nature of a method not previously exhibited in actual use is apt to be at best sterile, and at worst a positive source of prejudice which may subsequently hamper the process of investigation. (Taylor, 1903, p. 38)

This is probably doubly true for methods dealing with philosophical discourse because such methods do not attempt to expose any body of empirical fact. It seeks only to ask, what are the facts, and, are there any facts that are *the* facts?

Few facts are agreed upon universally in and of themselves. They require a system of interpretation. The system of interpretation employed greatly affects the so-called facts. Such systems of interpretation do not come from experience, because, for experience to be recognized as experience, some prior interpretation must be present (Bradley, 1908). Whitehead pointed out that, if one accepts only a record of uninterpreted experience, then one must ask a stone to write its autobiography. Thus no fact stands alone. It leans on other facts which support and develop it, and it leans on interpretation.

> The paradox of all this is that critical techniques, however genuine, may be a cul-de-sac. Criticism is itself a canon of judgement, and must therefore decide between facts that are important to it and facts that are not. (Drennen, 1962, p. 58)

Critical technique implies analysis, which, in turn, implies speculation and speculative doctrine. Thus, method, even critical method, is hoisted by its own logic. It does not precede philosophical inquiry but follows it. Philosophy does not settle on one method and then set out to work. On the contrary, rather than initiating inquiry, method is dependent on implicit philosophical judgments. Method is dictated by theory, not the other way around. This is a limitation because it necessitates the fact that "one looks for what one expects to find" (Whitehead, ed. Drennen, 1962, pp. 80–84). Fundamental attitudes precondition the decision to look for some facts and ignore others. Of all the attitudes toward procedure, two, rational and scientific, are most commonly used. Of these two, the limitations to scientific methodology are not necessarily fewer but they are easier to comprehend. These methods have concrete results born out of experimental data One working with this method is also able to exert near total control over the entire process of investigation. Of course, there are limitations even to this method. Although the method simply claims to describe fact, it still selects the facts that it describes. This process ultimately depends on an interpretation of a selection theory and, therefore, it is not a process of pure objectivity as is often claimed.

The limitations of a rational approach are twofold. Logic is claimed by the rationalist as his/her primary tool. There are those, though, who question this contention. Furthermore, they argue that the modern world has, through perceptual error, developed too many kinds of logic, each with its own presuppositions. Hence, one must ask, based on perception, what logic shall be used? The second limitation has to do with the criticism that the basic propositions sought through rationalism are neither universally accessible nor necessarily attainable. In other words, rationalism is simply a myth that "rational" men live by. The question then, "what deserves the title rational?", is not at all clear. These questions are limitations, but they are not barriers to adopting a rational method (Drennen, 1962). Jacques Maritain (1939) spoke of a rational approach (adopted by this book) which seeks to overcome these limitations. This approach is not one which asserts that the only method leading to truth is deductive reasoning. Maritain (1939) said that a human mind can comprehend much through its innate structure and then further advances deductively by a constant revitalization by experience. Mind, thus conceived, approaches reality in an open-handed fashion and attempts to read the character of ultimate reality. In other words, to try to move to the proper intellectual attitude toward ultimate reality. The mind does this through a metaphysical intuition that is amplified by both direct experience and deductive and objective control. The limitations of this paper are apparent, but any investigative work faces a number of limitations. It must be recognized, though, that since the methods of this book are different, then it is reasonable to expect that the limitations would differ also.

There are basically two procedures employed throughout this investigation. These procedures or methods are logical (according to the method by Maritain discussed above)—a critical comparative analysis—and compositional in nature. The analytical quality will be the attempt to analyze the fundamental assumptions of two counseling movements in an effort to discover the implications of these assumptions on counseling theory and to a lesser extent counseling practices. This analysis is being undertaken in order to determine the formal characteristics of two major counseling strategies in a philosophical context. By ascertaining such formal characteristics through analysis, it allows one to be able to view critically the various concepts and theories by referring to these characteristics as standards of ultimate reality (Taylor, 1903). This method is both nonempirical and noninductive. It is nonempirical in that it calls for an analysis of data in terms of its self-consistency and its internal character without imposing the observational quality of a rigorous empiricism on such analysis (Taylor, 1903). As previously stated, this type of analysis attempts to read and decipher the character of ultimate reality through the mind's innate structure amplified by direct experience and deductive control (Maritain, 1939). The nature of this method may be called a priori in that it proceeds entirely through the internal analysis of certain data and is, in procedure and result, independent of experience outside that direct experience that is the specific concern of this particular analysis (Taylor, 1903). In this case, this concern is the logical thread connecting antimetaphysics/environmentalism/B. F. Skinner and metaphysics/humanism/Viktor Frankl.

In terms of composition, this paper is organized along the lines of inductive logic. It proceeds from general to particular investigations. The first part is concerned with the broad general topic examining the character of the philosophic debate between metaphysics and antimetaphysics and the relationship of this debate to the present counseling conflict involving environmentalism and humanism. This is related to the concern of the second major thrust of this study, the identification and comparison of those specific fundamental assumptions which underlie humanism and environmentalism. In the third and most particular section of this book, the assumptions examined in part two will be examined in the light of the writings of two specific theorists in an attempt to examine the implications of these assumptions on the particular theoretical stances adopted by these two representative theorists. To a lesser extent these implications will also be examined in terms of the particular practices adopted by each theorist.

Chapter II

The Relationship of Humanism to Metaphysics and Environmentalism to Antimetaphysics

The metaphysical-antimetaphysical debate historically summarized in Chapter I is, of course, still unresolved. The presentation of the major arguments and counter arguments surrounding this question represents an attempt to familiarize counselors with these arguments and help them gain an understanding of the historical context and philosophical foundations of the conflict. Gaining a familiarity and understanding of this philosophic debate is of utmost importance to modern counselors. The importance derives from the fact that the environmentalism-humanism conflict in counseling finds its roots in the philosophic conflict. Whether or not they are aware of it, those in counseling supporting humanism as the proper direction for counseling are in a position of aligning themselves on the side of metaphysics. Those supporting environmentalism are aligned with antimetaphysics. The issue of humanism versus environmentalism in counseling is, in a large measure, simply a logical extension of the metaphysics versus antimetaphysics conflict in philosophy.

For much of its history, psychology and counseling have been dominated by two major theoretical forces. These two forces, environmental (encompassing all behavioral theories) and psychoanalytic, have generated the most concise theories, the most accepted methodologies, the bulk of scholastic research, and the most accepted teaching credentials within the field for the past 100 years. A relatively new discipline, the third force in counseling, has entered the field and since the 1950s has gained a certain discipleship and acceptance. This third force might be characterized as an amalgamation of those who subscribe to the validity of counseling but doubt the efficacy of psychoanalysis and environmental strategies to solve counseling problems. This movement is made up of gestaltists, phenomenologists, existentialists, and others espousing a more humanistic approach to counseling. From the time this humanistic force gained a bare minimum theoretical foothold in counseling thought, it found itself aligned against psychoanalysis and the environmental schools of counseling. This antithesis is apparent at all levels, theory, method, practice, and, most importantly, at the level of philosophical assumptions. In its most modern form, the major debate in counseling essentially concerns the antithetical nature of humanism and environmentalism. For this reason this particular book is not considering the role of psychoanalysis. The major task here is an examination of the modern counseling conflict at its most fundamental level. This examination will be undertaken in the following chapter. Before this examination is attempted, though, the attempt will be made to briefly examine the historical and philosophical context relating the counseling debate to the metaphysical-antimetaphysical debate.

The period of psychological thought known as classical behaviorism (1912–1930 approximately) was, ostensibly, an attempt to draw psychology into the modern realm of the "pure sciences" (especially classical Newtonian physics) and away from the realm of spiritualism, intuitiveness, and just plain guesswork. It was in Watson's words "an attempt to bury subjective subject matter" (Watson, cited by Koch, ed. Wann, 1964, p. 7). It was an effort to break with the then current theories and traditional concepts and bring a fresh start to psychology. In this fresh start "only such observations were to be considered admissible as can be made by independent observers upon the same object or event—exactly as in physics and chemistry" (Koch, ed. Wann, 1964, p. 8). This central thesis was usually advanced on methodological grounds, but early environmentalists offered the judgment (on metaphysical grounds) that "mind" or "consciousness" does not exist (Koch, ed. Wann, 1964). This advent of behavioral thought held that all lawful psychological statements could be expressed in terms of stimulus and response without having recourse to subjective thought. In an attempt to draw the "science" of psychology in line with the then recent discoveries in the science of physiology, behaviorists asserted "that processes formerly conceived as being determined primarily by the mind could be better understood if allocated mainly to physiological receptors, effectors, and their most direct nerve connections" (Koch, ed. Wann, 1964, p. 8).

These early behaviorists also rebelled against the traditional approach of psychology which stated that learning was a subsidiary of sensory and perceptual problems. Instead, they believed that a form of S-R associationism was basic to learning. Watson himself settled on the belief that the principle of conditioned reflex was the heart of the learning process. "By 1924, Watson was prepared to phrase all problems of learning in terms of conditioning" (Koch, ed. Wann, 1964, p. 9). The final foundation stone of the early behavioral movement was their pivotal belief in the strength of environmentalism as a shaper or determiner of all life, including, of course, human life. These precepts formed the cornerstones of early behaviorism. It was a movement designed to escape the stagnation of subjectivist introspection. which was prevalent in the psychology of that time by providing a staunch scientific decision-making procedure. This decision-making procedure (behaviorism) captured the loyalty of many students of this era, and Watson correctly reported the trend when he stated that "most of the younger psychologists realize that some such formulation as behaviorism is the only road leading to science" (Watson, 1924, p. viii).

In the 1920s and 30s behaviorism basically adhered to the cornerstones laid down by the classical behaviorists, but in this period certain additions were made that prompted the label "neo-behaviorism." The most important addition was a shift in the search for objectivity. At first behaviorists tried to guarantee objectivity of the descriptive concepts used for empirical data, but now the neo-behaviorists sought to continue this objectivity of method and also implement objectivism at the level of theory (Koch, ed. Wann, 1964).

> The idea was to insure that all elements of a system language be securely anchored by explicit linkages to antecedent independent and consequent dependent variables, and, in general, to effect a point-for-point correspondence of the logical properties of systematic formulations of psychology with those of psychology's traditional emulation model, physics. (Koch, ed. Wann, 1964, p. 10)

Humanists of today claim that, in order to achieve this, past psychology did not go directly to physics. Instead, it turned to certain "middlemen" to receive its marching orders. These middlemen were philosophers of science (especially logical positivists) and physical science methodologists. These philosophers and methodologists propagated a view, based on a rational reconstruction of a few formulations in theoretical physics, of a detailed model of a scientific enterprise which came to be called the hypothetico-deductive method (Koch, ed. Wann, 1964). The greatest sources of philosophic impact in the psychology of this period were primarily logical positivism and a form of neopragmatism.

Koch (ed. Wann, 1964) claimed that, with a few minor modifications, the modern behaviorist position is remarkably similar to the early days of the movement. The modern behaviorist still holds to the general foundations laid by his predecessors and with very little effort these foundations can be traced back to the philosophical foundations of the antimetaphysical position. The idea that there is a marked connection between the antimetaphysical movement and the environmental movement is perhaps nothing new. Other authors have made this same connection. But most people, including counselors, have tended toward a study of theories and methods and away from the basic philosophic assumptions which spawned those particular theories and methods. No less a behavioral authority than B. F. Skinner says that stories of early behaviorists and their foundational pronouncements are irrelevant. Skinner (ed. Wann, 1964) made a distinction between "behaviorism as a philosophy of science and the science of behavior" (p. 42). He (ed. Wann, 1964) further insisted that "behaviorism is not to be identified with logical positivism" (p. 42). Skinner claimed that it only causes confusion when behaviorism is studied at its philosophical levels.

> The science of behavior is moving very rapidly and powerfully and it does not need this kind of philosophical justification... (It justifies itself by its success in dealing with the subject matter. (Skinner, ed. Wann, 1964)

Critics of behaviorism claim that Skinner is saying that there is a science of behavior whether or not there is a useful philosophy of science of behaviorism; thus making philosophy unnecessary. Many humanists believe that this argument cannot be justified by any rational means. They also claim that this unwillingness to study its own fundamental precepts causes environmentalism to be weak at both the level of theory and practice.

When one examines the basic tenets of .environmentalism and antimetaphysics, especially as antimetaphysics reveals itself in its positivistic phase, a very close kinship is discovered, regardless of Skinner's claim to the contrary. This kinship is perhaps most noticeable in the so-called "objective view" of the true scientist. Previously, it was stated that the fundamental key for modern antimetaphysicians is the belief that all true knowledge is verifiable through sensate observation. In contrasting this position with environmentalism's pronouncement that the only observations considered admissible are those made by independent observers upon the same object or event, one can see that this behavioral commitment is a simple restatement of the positivistic antimetaphysical principle of verifiability. Watson's studies of classical conditioning and Skinner's work in reinforcement theory echo the positivist commitment to observable verifiability. In Watson's famous experiment where he struck a loud noise on a metal bar whenever a small child touched a fuzzy stuffed animal, thus conditioning the child to cry and be afraid of fuzzy stuffed animals even in the absence of the loud terrifying noise, he based his conclusions totally on observable reactions. He could verify the results of his conditioning techniques by observing outward changes in his subjects. Results gleaned from behavioral experiments using "Skinner boxes" or mazes reflect this same interest in verifiable quantification. The time a mouse spends "solving" a maze is both an observable and a measurable quantity. This principle of observability and sensate verification forms the basis of all environmental experimentation just as it forms the key principle of positivistic philosophy.

Environmentalists, like the positivists, also seek to extend this principle of objectivity into the area of theory as well as method. The goal for behaviorists and antimetaphysicians is the same, "to bury subjective subject matter" (Watson, cited by Koch, ed. Wann, 1964), p. 7). This objectivist epistemology is fundamental to both positions. Koch (ed. Wann, 1964) stated that the "criterion of 'firm anchorage' of theoretical concepts in explicit functional relations to antecedent and consequent 'observables'" (p. 15) is a logical extension of the positivist position that all knowledge is sensory in nature and verifiable in principle. In this way it is inferred that explanatory concepts are to be unequivocally linked to observables, and therefore there will no longer be a fear of irresponsible subjectivist constructions based on the whim of the theorists or practitioner (Koch, ed. Wann, 1964).

The basic antimetaphysical contention that the method of natural science is the only road to knowledge has also been adopted by environmentalism. Hull and other behaviorists' advocacy of the hypothetico-deductive method for psychology is based on this positivist dictum. This method is an extension of the belief that "a properly rule-regulated scientific work is self-corrective" (Koch, ed. Wann, 1964, p. 11) and is viewed by behaviorists as a more or less sure-fire instrumentality for scientific advance. This fervent drive toward quantification is seen in both positivism and behaviorism. The adoption of the scientific method seems, to environmentalists, a built-in guarantor of success. It gives a standard method, a "defining experiment" to infer postulates from experimental evidence. "In briefest terms, the method selects or designs a series of experiments, the empirical variables of which would represent the theoretical variables in question, thus objectifying the theoretical process" (Koch, ed. Wann, 1964, pp. 15–16). This procedure should show that the problems of subjectivistic psychology can find an objective resolution. This is an echo of A. J. Ayer and Morris Lazerowitz's positivistic contention that there is no knowledge with which one or other of the natural sciences does not deal; no knowledge over and above scientific knowledge.

The antimetaphysical and environmental positions find points of commonality in areas other than objectivity, preeminence of sensate knowledge, acceptance of the scientific method as the basis for all knowledge, and the verifiability principle. The concepts of relativity and utility also overlap in these positions. Much of the previously mentioned material concerning the emphasis of relativity and utility in antimetaphysics is also applicable to modern environmentalism. Many humanists make much of the idea of the primacy of the self with the implied reliance on an ultimate Self as final and absolute authority. Environmentalists deny such a relationship and "feel that individual self-hood can be described in thoroughly behavioristic fashion" (Butler, 1951, p. 441). Individual will is not seen as an efficient cause for change when this will is based on absolute or ultimate principles. Rather, environmentalists, like antimetaphysicians, think of the individual as a concrete social phenomenon whose acts are relatively based on the social stream of interactivity. In other words, the individual is a product of a relative society, not a self-determiner based on absolute principles. The individual can only react to society, and as society changes so does the individual. This idea is very similar to the pragmatic belief of antimetaphysics that all things flow and change and no principles are absolute or remain the same (Butler, 1951). Metaphysics and humanism have a frame of reference predisposed to the inquiry into the absolute principles of reason. From this philosophical inquiry into these general absolute principles, more specific items of knowledge can possibly be deduced. Antimetaphysics and environmentalism are leery of all generalizations. Their frame of reference is always sense-perceptual experience based on utilitarian concepts of society (Butler, 1951, pp. 446–447). Gordon Allport (1955) termed this the man as a purely reactive being theory, and along with other humanists he strongly disagreed with the mechanistic and purely animalistic overtones of such a theory. Humanists claim that, by following this line of thought to its natural conclusion, counseling becomes merely the espousal of certain techniques designed to fit society's utilitarian concepts. Most humanistic theories state that this path chosen by the environmentalists leads to a highly manipulatory set of beliefs concerning human nature and emphasizes technique over sound theory.

Environmentalism in counseling is perhaps the most technique oriented of all theoretical positions. This reliance on technique has its roots in the positivistic doctrine of relativity and emphasis on the experimental method. This method reflects the pragmatic doctrine that everything changes.

> One of the main features of pragmatism...is that it is a dynamic philosophy. In contrast to philosophers like Plato and Descartes who adopt the standpoint of pure intelligence in contemplation of the eternal verities, the pragmatists put themselves in the position of an inquirer adapting himself to

> and helping to modify a*changing* world. This is a point which has always to be borne in mind, if their work is to be sympathetically understood. (Ayer, 1968, p. 5–6)

Sometimes the changes are smooth, but often the changes demand that something new or different be done. At times of change, new directions are determined, thus affecting the subsequent flow of experience. These new directions are neither right nor wrong. They are simply new. The new directions are arrived at by observing (objectively verifying) the facts which comprise a particular (relative) unit of experience. The cue for further action is suggested by the objective observation of the data. This observation yields patterns of action and analyses of these patterns become the hypotheses on which to act. The final step in this method is the testing of these hypotheses. This experimental method of environmentalism yields two things:

> knowledge, to the limited extent of a sense of the particular way of acting which is acceptable in a particular unit of experience, and value, to the extent that there is action and judgment where something is done which yields changes and brings needed results. (Butler, 1951, pp. 450–451)

Both the relative and utilitarian qualities of positivism and pragmatism are easily seen in this environmental method. Skinner (ed. Wann, 1964) claimed that these "techniques based on empiricism are more advantageous than absolute pronouncements based on philosophy or logic" (p. 84).

The overlapping characteristics of antimetaphysics and environmentalism form the defining criteria of these movements. Since in almost every case the defining criteria are the same, it would lead one to conclude that on some levels the positions are similar, if not identical, in nature. The contention has been made early in this book that there is indeed a relationship between antimetaphysics and counseling's environmentalism. The similarity of defining criteria would seem to support this contention. The points of similarity between environmentalism and antimetaphysics are particularly evident in the following characteristics: The method of natural science is the only road to knowledge, true knowledge is verifiable only through objective observation (in counseling perhaps the term behavioral change could be used in place of "true knowledge"), knowledge comes from the senses only, and science does not and should not deal with abstract speculation or principles of ultimacy.

This brief summary of environmental and antimetaphysical characteristics clearly states their basic position on fundamental issues and this summary provides the opportunity to turn to the metaphysical point of view and examine the position it takes on these same fundamental issues. There is such a direct antipathy between the metaphysical and antimetaphysical position that it would be fair to state that the defining criteria of the metaphysical position is the exact opposite of the antimetaphysical position. As previously mentioned, metaphysics claims that the method of natural science is a way to knowledge, but it is not exclusively the only way. One certainly gains knowledge through the senses, but this is by no means the only conduit to knowledge, and finally it is indeed the business of science and philosophy to investigate abstractions and questions of ultimacy. In fact, it will be remembered that the working definition of metaphysics employed in this study is the attempt to find the correct intellectual attitude toward ultimate reality. Metaphysical arguments supporting these defining criteria have previously been cited. Counseling's humanistic forces employ these same arguments against environmentalism.

In addition to the method of natural science, humanists find other avenues of knowledge. One such method is through phenomenological intuiting. This is an intense concentration on, or attentive internal gaze at, certain phenomena. Another method of humanism is through analyzing or finding various constituents of phenomena and their relation. Describing is an account of intuited and analyzed phenomena so it can be understood by others (Spiegelberg, 1960). These methods of gaining knowledge are irreconcilable with the precepts of environmentalism, but humanists claim that a "mere investigation of facts alone does not yield knowledge and psychology cannot merely be a collection of correlated facts" (Misiak & Sexton, 1973, p. 13).

In many other areas the defining criteria of humanism exhibit the same basic characteristics as metaphysics.

> Its protest is directed against the entire orientation of psychology and philosophy since Hobbes and Locke, against its Newtonian and Darwinian models of man, and against its mechanistic, deterministic, and reductionistic character. (Misiak & Sexton, 1973, p. 115)

Humanism rejects much of environmentalism's work with the lower animals and its implicit statement of kinship between the lower animals and humanity and instead stresses the special characteristics and capacities which make humans uniquely different from these lower animals. Humanistic counseling rejects the environmental notion that one can make objective observations of lower animals (a mouse in a maze for example) and go directly from this observation to imply total relevancy for human behavior. They say that the actions of lower animals and humans in given situations are not interchangeable. Rogers (cited in Misiak & Sexton, 1973) stated that humanists "are concerned with the whole spectrum of human behavior and human behavior is, in some significant ways, something more than the behavior of our laboratory animals" (p. 103). Humanists believe in Bugental's (cited in Misiak & Sexton, 1973) contention that environmental psychology as it has descended from positivistic philosophies is reductionistic and mechanistic, and has reduced humanity to either a large white rat or a very slow computer. Humanists contend that environmentalism emphasizes humanity's continuity with the animal world while humanism focuses on humanity's unique differences.

The focus on this uniqueness can be seen in humanism's four major characteristics: (a) The center of attention is on the experiencing *person*, not on the experience itself; (b) the emphasis is placed on the distinctively human (as opposed to animal) qualities, such as choice, creativity, valuation, and self-realization; (c) opposition to a primary emphasis on objectivity at the expense of significance; and (d) a concern with ultimacy in terms of humanity's existence, knowledge, dignity, and worth (Misiak & Sexton, 1973). It is obvious that these characteristics show a basic kinship to the precepts of the philosophical position of metaphysics. The fact that their primary characteristics and concerns have such a high degree of similarity leads one to acknowledge a very close relationship between humanism and metaphysics. It also follows that, since the defining criteria of environmentalism and antimetaphysics overlap and the defining criteria of humanism and metaphysics also coincide, then the overlap in the basic arguments between them would also be present. This indeed seems to be the case.

Environmentalism and antimetaphysics subscribe to the reductionistic canons of the inductive scientific method. Humanists and metaphysicians both claim to argue for a system not limited to this single method. The idea that, if one continues to pare away the qualities of an object one by one, one will eventually get at the thing itself is, to humanists and metaphysicians, a false doctrine. They see no benefit in trying to deal with some object, problem, or part of experience in isolation from the rest of experience. "Every object, every problem, every part of experience is what it is just because of its relation to the whole" (Butler, 1966, p. 65). By divorcing things from their relationships to wholes and attempting to study them at their most bare level of specialization, one can only arrive at a very antiseptic and often erroneous conclusion. "True knowledge...can only be achieved by seeing things in their relationship to the whole" (Butler, 1966, p. 65).

The relationship of parts to wholes also points out another facet of this debate. The environmental and antimetaphysical position states that the senses are the only path to knowledge. Conversely, humanists and metaphysicians say that, as in the above illustration, sometimes one's senses can be deceived and that knowing is more than sensory input. As far back as Plato and Kant, the metaphysical (and hence today's humanism) position has held that pure sensation is a chaotic process with all kinds of sensory stimulations being passively received by the mind. It is the mind, the self, that gives coherence to the sensate material. The world of sensation is only meaningful because it is refracted through a perceiving mind or a perceptive self. "It is like music after being refracted through the soul and instrument of the musician" (Butler, 1966, p. 61). The primacy of the self then is a key position held by metaphysicians and humanists but not by environmentalists and antimetaphysicians. This primacy of self insists that the path to knowledge is not purely sensational, objective, or verifiable. It is personal and subjective also. Humanists claim that they acknowledge the value of objective science. They can live with it and join in its advancement but only on the terms of admitting the superiority of the personal self over scientific achievement.

Humanists believe that psychology, and thus counseling also, made a serious mistake in its historical base when it adopted the tenets of positivism, antimetaphysics, and Newtonian physics as its role model. They feel that this historical attempt to bring psychology into the realm of science and out of the realm of metaphysical philosophy has had a great effect on modern psychology. Before the advent of humanism, almost all American psychologists were exposed in their training to the positivistic, pragmatic, a philosophical doctrine of environmentalism (Misiak & Sexton, 1973). Humanists now argue that this doctrine which forms environmentalism's base is in error. Humanists contend that the environmental defense is based on even shakier ground than its philosophical forebearer, antimetaphysics. At least the defense of antimetaphysics has evolved and changed over the years in an attempt to cope with metaphysical counterarguments. But environmentalism has continued to pattern itself after a natural science that is said to be unsupportable even by natural scientists.

> The picture of scientific method now beginning to emerge among physicists, other natural scientists, many philosophers of science, and others challenges the environmental conception of science...at virtually every point. (Koch, ed. Wann, 1964, p. 21)

Humanists continue to argue that the environmental idea of replicability of findings and reliability of prediction based totally on fixed linkages with objective indicators and within a wholly stated context of immutable rules is being refuted not only by themselves but by natural scientists as well. The rule saturated conception of science was dominant in science 20 to 30 years ago but has since been abandoned by everyone but psychology's environmentalists. In science and the philosophy of science not a single plank in the old positivistic-neopragmatic scaffolding remains unaltered (Koch, ed. Wann, 1965). Such renowned positivistic thinkers as Carnap and Zeigh have retreated from many of their earlier positions. As early as 1956, Carnap pointed out that

> a person's awareness of his own state of imagining, feeling, etc. must be recognized as a kind of observation, in principle not different from external observation, and therefore as a legitimate source of knowledge. (pp. 70–71)

> Carnap and other positivists have liberalized much of their meaning criteria out of all recognition. . . yet very little of this has penetrated into psychology. (Koch, ed. Wann, 1964, p. 25)

Koch (ed. Wann, 1964) further claimed that environmentalists still draw sustenance from a theory of definition (and more generally of science) that has been largely abandoned even by its originators. Humanists feel that environmentalists have avoided coming to grips with those conflicts and contradictions which caused their natural science role models to change some of their basic ideas.

Another humanist complaint is the belief that environmentalists have been very restrictive in their problem selection. This policy of evading and ignoring certain subject matter has gradually over the years given way to a policy of actually denying the existence of this subject matter.

> Environmentalists have shied away from investigations, even of behavior, when it is under the control of complex or labile internal factors and have concentrated on dependent variable indicators of a type dictated more by methodological caution than problematic relevance. (Koch, ed. Wann, 1965, p. 31)

In its attempt to be ultrascientific, psychology has denied subjectivity and attempted to walk in the totally objective steps of Newtonian physics. Yet most agree that this model is a false one—"The worst misunderstanding would be that psychology be influenced to model itself after a physics which is not there any more, which has been quite outdated" (Oppenheimer, 1956, p. 134). Carl Rogers (ed. Wann, 1964) described this fascination with scientific objectivity and verifiability as constricting.

> To limit oneself to consideration of externally observable behavior, to rule out of consideration the whole universe of inner meanings, of purposes, of the inner flow of experiencing, seems to me to be closing our eyes to great areas which confront us when we look at the human world. (p. 119).

He (ed. Wann, 1964) also stated that the idea that science is totally impersonal and carries itself forward without the subjective person of the scientist being involved is an illusion. By following environmental dictates, humanity can only be a machine, a complicated but, nonetheless, understandable machine "which we can learn to manipulate with greater and greater skill until he thinks the thoughts, moves in the directions, and behaves in the ways selected for him" (Rogers, ed. Wann, 1964, p. 129). Humanists declare that it is their contention that humans are not machines but are persons and selves in the process of creating in large part their own selfhood. A self who creates meaning in life and embodies a dimension of subjective freedom. Wittgenstein's (1922) antimetaphysical rule stating that whereof one cannot speak, thereof one must be silent, is adopted by environmentalism but stoutly denied by humanists. Humanists say they seek after unknowns in order to make them known. If ultimate concepts are knowable, and humanists and metaphysicians believe they are, then they deserve to be studied, even if to do so means employing subjective means.

The philosophical assumptions underlying environmentalism and humanism will be examined in a following section and a common thread will be evident. This common thread is the same one that has been previously examined in establishing a relationship between philosophical debates and counseling debates. The preceding sections have tried to enlighten counselors to this important relationship for two reasons: (a) in the belief that, by understanding the historical and philosophical context of the philosophical debate, one would be better able to understand the basic contentions of each side of the counseling debate and be better able to engage in decision-making procedures; and (b) also because this metaphysics-antimetaphysics relationship is extended into the fundamental assumptions of each counseling position (humanism identifying with metaphysics and environmentalists identifying with antimetaphysics). If one is to truly understand the specific philosophical assumptions of the two counseling positions, one must see them in their relationship to the larger philosophical debate. As was earlier stated, this is done not to resolve the debate, but to present to counselors the historical basis for what has been referred to as the most significant and far reaching debate (between environmentalism and humanism) in the present and future scene of American psychology and counseling (Misiak & Sexton, 1973). Presenting the metaphysical-antimetaphysical debate and showing its progenitor relationship to counseling's humanistic-environmental debate reflects the belief that counselors could better understand, and make more thoughtful decisions, by examining and coming to grips with the philosophical genesis of their own position.

The major intent of the remainder of this book will be to isolate the specific philosophical and metaphysical assumptions underlying the two major positions of modern counseling, environmentalism and humanism. In Chapter III these assumptions will be identified, compared, and analyzed in terms of similarities and differences. Also, an attempt will be made to investigate the role these assumptions play in the general formation of environmental and humanistic counseling theory, method, and practice. Chapters IV and V will then examine the writings of a representative theorist of each movement and attempt to trace the relationship and lineal descent of the philosophical assumptions of Chapter III and the translation of these assumptions into an end product in terms of a counseling philosophy, theory, method, and practice as exemplified in the explicit and implicit writings of both representative theorists.

Chapter III

Fundamental Principles of Humanism and Environmentalism

The philosophic debate between metaphysics and antimetaphysics can be seen as something of a common thread running throughout every aspect of this particular investigation. The specific philosophic assumptions of humanism and environmentalism to be identified in this chapter will, in most cases, also reflect the oppositional character and influence of the metaphysical-antimetaphysical conflict. The assumptions underlying humanistic counseling theory and practice will show (with some minor differences) a basic kinship to the metaphysical position outlined previously. The relationship between counseling's environmental schools of thought and antimetaphysical positions will also be evident. The ontological, epistemological, and axiological bases of humanism and environmentalism are vastly different. This difference is not the result of coincidence. Rather, these differences represent the continuation of the metaphysical-antimetaphysical debate and, by inference, seem to indicate that the process of bringing about human behavior change is deeply intertwined with this philosophic conflict. This means that the goals, methods, and criteria of evaluation developed and utilized by various theoretical approaches to counseling are primarily drawn from philosophic assumptions laid down long ago by those carrying on the metaphysical-antimetaphysical debate.

Ontology

The ontological concerns of environmentalism have never played a major role in the aggrandizement of the movement. Environmentalism has always had an object (rather than subject) centered view of being. Historically, this concentration on objectivism has virtually guaranteed that environmentalism would not possess a thoroughly delineated theory of being. Koch (ed. Wann, 1964) noted that "the lack of respect for ontology has remained pretty much constant throughout the history of behaviorism [environmentalism]" (p. 32). Although it is true that environmentalism has not been concerned with ontological problems, a few key ontological pronouncements can be isolated which are consistent with the general tone of the theory. Barclay's (1968) groundbreaking work in this area lists several key environmental ontological beliefs. Koch (ed. Wann, 1964) and other scholars interested in both philosophy and psychology earlier noted a basic similarity in the philosophic principles of environmentalism and antimetaphysics and Barclay's work seems to reinforce their findings. First of all, Barclay (1968) noted that the environmentalists see humans as "an evolved animal whose functions and behavior can only be understood in terms of physicalistic forces or conditions" (p. 23). Thus conceived, humanity is determined and shaped by forces extraneous to its own subjective personhood. The amount of control one has over these forces varies somewhat within the environmental movement. At one extreme are those environmentalists (Farber, Dollard and Miller, and others) who claim that mankind has ceased to be a complete product of the environment and has not been totally determined since leaving the caves for the final time. These so-called moderate environmentalists believe that through science human beings can create their own environment. At the other extreme are the more radical environmentalists who believe that humanity was, is, and always will be merely a creation of a particular environment. Michael and Myerson (1962) stated that the single most important thrust of environmental thought is a

> behavior system [that] attempts to specify, without reference to unobservable, hypothetical inner-determining agents [subjectivism], the conditions and the process by which the environment controls human behavior. (p. 383)

B. F. Skinner's (1948) *Walden Two* serves, in its entirety, as a champion of the more radical (man is completely determined) stance. In *Walden II*, Skinner outlined a society constructed entirely along the lines of intentional conditioning techniques. In this imaginary society, a particular environment is created and all members, especially the young, are conditioned to react "properly" to the structured environment.

Following the line of reasoning developed in *Walden II*, environmentalists hold that it is not a question of whether or not more subjective procedures could modify the determining forces of the environment. Rather, they state that such subjective methods are incapable of being evaluated by the scientific method and must therefore be treated as nonexistent. Zax and Klein (1960) maintained that without an observable cause and effect relationship, subjective forces, such as insight or self-understanding, could not be considered to alter man's determined nature or bring about any ultimate behavior change. Michael and Meyerson (1962) echoed this theme by asserting that observable behavior is the only important variable in the entire counseling process. Subjective methods are not observable and therefore cannot be considered in any way to alter the basic contention that humanity is, by and large, a determined product of the environment. Viewed in this deterministic fashion, reality can only be approached in what Descartes labeled the "Res Extensa," the world of external phenomena. It is in this world that all of environmentalism's ontological beliefs are born, because this is the only world where any meaningful, observable, and verifiable philosophy of science can operate. Humanity, like any other animal, finds its being in this world. This being is shaped by external phenomenon, forces, and laws that exist beyond any human control. Mankind "possesses no a priori characteristics other than his biological structure" (Barclay, 1971, p. 393). Thus, "man is not an active cause in the world" (Butler, 1951, p. 457). Humanity is rather a factor caused by the world.

In order to understand environmental ontology, one must come to the realization that the environmentalists have been primarily concerned with defining and specifying what reality is not, rather than what it is. Their basic contention is that the ultimate quality of reality (if indeed there even is such a thing) cannot be known and therefore is not and should not be of concern. There simply are no universal abstractions or universal ideas. Thus stripped of any absolute or ultimate nature, reality can be explained as a series of changes detectable solely through the physical senses. This is precisely the environmental position. Viewed in this way, reality is limited to strictly definable phenomena which exist in a world of observable and quantifiable experimental manipulation and statistical inference (Barclay, 1968). This means that the scientific method becomes the sole criterion of philosophic clarity and, in turn, the sole criterion of clarity in the counseling theories and methods that stem from this philosophy. This leaves little room for any conception of an all embracing reality which serves as a background for every human experience and human activity (Butler, 1951). Environmentalism puts all its emphasis on the changing nature of society and no emphasis at all on any absolute cosmology. "The reality we [man] live in, the world of sensation, of change, of growth, and death is the only world we can intelligently manage in human discourse" (Barclay, 1971, p. 395). All transactions between this reality and the individual must take place in a realm governed by the physical senses, because these senses represent the only way of being in contact with this reality—this world of physical phenomena. "Events come and go, one set of circumstances is replaced by another, and in turn by another. Nothing is static or permanent" (Butler, 1951, p. 454). Human beings can often recognize the changing circumstances and can modify the environmental constraints producing a particular set of circumstances. This environmental manipulation is the key;

understanding absolute principles is said to be a waste of time. Environmental theory and methodologies are born in this single clear distinction: Humanity does not have freedom of choice as such and the flow of environmental events cannot be changed. But people can find room in the flow of events to engage in experimental activities, based on the precepts of the scientific method, designed to alter the future directions in which events flow (Butler, 1951). This belief rests at the heart of environmental reasoning. Though not as minutely detailed as environmental epistemology, these ontological concerns form the basis for both the epistemological and axiological canons of the position. A reality of this type pictures humankind as just another entity existing on the evolutionary scale. Humanity is largely a determined product of the environment although to be sure they do exert somewhat more control on that environment than most of their evolutionary companions. Humanity, in this view, is not unique. It is discernible and decipherable in the same way as all of reality, through the physical senses and the verifiability of the scientific method.

Humanist ontological concerns stand in stark contrast to environmental concerns. In a later section these differences will be further explored, but even the neophyte counselor could not fail immediately to recognize the oppositional nature of the respective ontological pronouncements. The humanist position is more conscious of and devoted to its ontological underpinnings. Therefore, humanist ontology is a more clearly delineated and distinct body of thought. One explanation for this is the idea that a fairly substantial portion of humanist ontology is closely related to the philosophical position of idealism. This philosophical position has existed as a distinct body of reasoning for a long period, thus, historically, allowing the position to be quite specific in its proposals. In other words, idealism has been extant long enough for the position to be refined and intellectually polished to a product having a high degree of consensus at its most basic levels. Since humanist ontology, in many ways, draws some of its principles from idealist ontology, it [humanism] has been the beneficiary of the years of study of idealistic precepts. Also because of this relationship, it has a fairly consistent ontological base.

Humanism professes to believe in the environmental pronouncements about the objective nature of reality, but they say that even though this certainly exists, it [objectivism] cannot explain the specialized nature of human reality. Understanding humanity, the world, the universe, and ultimate reality can only come about by acknowledging that a true picture of reality is possible through subjectivism. In this view, reality consists of both an external (objective) and an internal (subjective) dimension. Those holding this view believe that it is simple logic that dictates that the subjective or internal portion of reality should have greater priority. As far back as the "Cartesian Cogito" (I think, therefore I am) and earlier, some people have taken the organized position that one can know the internal realm of reality better than the external realm, because items in the external dimension (objective phenomena) can only be experienced indirectly in the light of internal experiences (subjectivism). "Thus what we know of external reality, that is, the world of scientific investigation and factual knowledge, is filtered through the mediation of internal experiencing" (Barclay, 1971, p. 308). This concentration on subjective reality is a primary point of humanist ontology.

This subjective reality is the conscious or unconscious belief that all people seem to believe themselves to be real existent beings and not transitory illusions, dreams, or fancies (Butler, 1951). Royce (1919) explained this subjective quality of reality when he wrote that

> with the reality of the self seen as the most self-evident fact any of us can experience, many find then that the nature of the rest of existence is strongly implied... Whenever a man tries to proclaim his view about the world, he may insist that the world must have any number of possible characteristics; but no matter which he upholds, it is important to note that it is always *his* ideal which is attributed to the world. If he insists, for example, that the world must be regarded as independent of our minds [non-subjective] because that is the only wholesome view, then he "announces" an explicitly subjective theory, since he defines the nature of reality in terms of his subjective ideal of wholesomeness. (Royce, 1919, p. 237)

Royce (1919) also wrote that our views of the world are always "conceptual constructs because we interpret the universe as the expression of the more or less conscious demands of the rational self" (p. 243).

> The argument of intelligibility is another instance of selfhood providing us with a strong suggestion as to the nature of reality. The world of self is a world of intelligence; in it there are qualities, meanings, and values. It is suicidal to divorce these values from the only metaphysic that makes their validity intelligible. (Butler, 1951, p. 197).

A second major consideration of humanistic ontology is the belief in the existence and supreme importance of an individual self. This primacy of the self is reflected throughout humanism. Finding out about this self represents a key goal toward which humanists strive. But the foundational point of humanism rests not on finding out *what* the self is; it rests on acknowledging *that* the self is. If the self is nonexistent or if it is identical with the body or a mere unit of society, as environmentalists suppose, then the fact that it *is* has no special meaning. But if the self (as humanists propose) is not totally identifiable with the body or with society, if it exists as that essence which makes the human relationship to reality a special case over and above evolutionary or environmental constraints, then it opens the way for an interpretation of ultimate meanings in all reality. Viewed in this way, the self becomes the specialized interpreter of ultimate reality (a view of such a self in a religious study would, no doubt, necessitate the labeling of such a self as a "soul." A philosophical view would bring about the term "mind" to replace the term self. But because of a desire to avoid [at least at this time] such religious and philosophical "power words" and also because the term self is most used in counseling literature [rather than soul or mind], this book will continue to employ the term self to denote that specialized, subjective realm recognized in humanistic doctrines.)

The acknowledgement of this primacy of the self leads humanists to what they see as the next logical step. Since there is a self and since this self represents the best chance to interpret ultimate reality, this strongly implies that ultimate reality is a self also. In order for the world to be capable of interpretation, it must be tuned to the same key as the self (Butler, 1966). Therefore it cannot be either totally material or totally mechanical. It must be closely linked to the self or it would be beyond interpretation. If it is beyond interpretation, then there can be no philosophy and no science because then all would be chaos. This does not seem to be the case. For while the world and reality in general still has many mysteries, it does seem amenable to some interpretation and this means being tuned to the same key as the interpreter (Butler, 1951).

This line of thought dictates that the consideration of an individual self as an isolated, totally independent thinker does not do justice to reality. Rather, this self, though individuated and unique, exists as a part of a whole. This self is one individual unit in the whole of reality.

> Therefore, what goes on in the self is not only an evidence of the nature of the individual self but is also fully representative of the nature of that reality of which the self is a part. (Butler, 1966, p. 44).

The importance of this idea of self cannot be overemphasized in the humanist position. It represents the focal point of other humanistic ontological ideas, epistemologies, and axiologies. The character of this self can be summarized as follows: it is the first and foremost interpreter of objective phenomena; it is the prime reality of individual experience; ultimate reality is a self; the individual, as part of a nonmechanized, nondetermined ultimate reality, is then itself nonmechanized and nondetermined and possesses the freedom essential to self-determination (Butler, 1966). The ultimate goal of this self-determination is not to deal passively with experiential material but rather to reach and grasp the essences, the meanings of these experiences as they appear in consciousness. This self represents the only way to divest meanings from our experiences (Spiegelberg, 1960).

Plato (cited in Butler, 1951) talked about the existence of ideas that are so important, so real and enduring that objects of sense are fleeting when compared to them. Physical objects are thus only embodiments of the ideas that they represent. Some ideas (questions of ultimacy) are not capable of representation in physical form and therefore are to be perceived, not through physical experience, but rather through ideational abstraction. The human self is unique in this ability to deal with abstract thoughts. Since these thoughts are not capable of representation in physical form, it is a mistake and an impossibility to attempt to decipher them through the physical senses. Abstractions are not quantifiable or verifiable through the senses or the scientific method. Such abstractions can be deciphered only if one were to approach them at their proper starting point in thought. Since the self is the only self-evident reality, it represents the necessary base for all understanding. To start from any other point, such as the physical world, is to make a huge question-begging leap. "We must begin with the known, not the unknown, and the knowledge of the self is the only immediate knowledge that any of us have" (Butler, 1951, p. 138). This self is that piece of reality from which all knowledge moves outward. It is easy to see that Carl Rogers (ed. Wann, 1964) incorporates this humanist ontology in his counseling theory. Rogers sees the self as inner-directed rather than shaped by external forces (an all-knowing counselor, for example). Rogers is a good example because his theory rests almost totally on humanism's ontological pronouncements concerning the nature of the self, but all humanistic counseling theorists stress, to one degree or another, the importance of a subjective knower—a self—in each of their respective counseling approaches.

Denying the reality of such a self reduces humanity to the simple level of biological order. Humanists certainly acknowledge a biological order but they also affirm the reality of a self (individual and unique) over and above biological considerations. This affirmation makes humanity a higher entity and not a simple, predictable, determined biological process. William Urban (1930) summarized this controversy of the self as follows:

> We are trying to decide whether or not we are merely high-grade simians or whether we are sons of God—in more philosophical terms, whether our intelligence, reason, and all these terms connote, are really biological adaptations or have also a transcendental meaning or status. (p. 371).

As earlier stated, being, for the environmentalist, is characterized by a posteriori development, but being for the humanist (excluding most forms of existentialism; this will be discussed in more detail later) is a question of an a priori structure or an essence. This essence, from the Latin word essentia, meaning "to be," forms the individual, real, or ultimate nature of a thing (in this case human beings). Attributing an a priori essence to humanity rather than an a posteriori existence, removes humankind from a totally determined reality. This essence makes humans as much a creator as a creation. It makes being more than a biological process and more than an accident of experience. Thus human beings are not created through their experiences. Rather, through their essence, through the ultimate nature of being, humanity, in many ways, creates its own experiences. In counseling, this means that the ultimate responsibility to act (to get better) resides in one's own essential self. A belief in this a priori essential nature of humanity causes humanistic counseling theory to remove a great deal of the responsibility for progress from the therapist and places it squarely on the shoulders of the subject of counseling.

The investigation of the human essence must not be restricted to the strictly observable canons of the physical sciences. This would eliminate all subjective knowledge and make it impossible to examine the ultimate qualities of humankind. As was previously mentioned, the term objective reality is a bit of a misnomer. In one way or another objective reality is, mentally, a reflection of what the mind (the knowing self) perceives. The only way to understand the ultimate nature of humanity is to make use of humankind's own subjective being. Investigations concerning humanity surely take place through objective procedures based on law, order, and causality, but primarily such investigations depend on the subjective agent or the knowing person (Barclay, 1968). Brentano (1902) went so far as to say that the entire subject matter of psychology and of all humanity is subjective phenomenon. Many humanists are unwilling to go this far, but every humanist insists that the unique human subjective dimension cannot be dismissed. Objective quantification is important, but human beings are best studied at the level of their own fundamental being—the self. This cannot be accomplished without delving into the subjective domain. Humanistic ontology is an attempt "to probe the nature of the self through consciousness and the a priori components of consciousness" (Barclay, 1968, p. 37). This ontology is reflected in humanistic counseling thought. It reflects an organized search of the invariant structure which discovers, channels, and attaches meaning to psychic phenomena. The basis for this position is a subjectivity characterized by the transcendental thesis that all existence is the result of a priori structure. Counseling is related to this essentialistic philosophy because its methods and goals are designed to probe and understand the inner essential structure of humanity (Barclay, 1968).

Earlier an assertion was made to the effect that humanism, as an integral, self-enclosed counseling movement, lacked the cohesiveness of the environmental position. It should be noted that in examining humanistic ontology this lack of cohesiveness is readily apparent. Two of the major forces, phenomenology and existentialism, existing within the humanism framework have some fairly sharp differences concerning ontology. In fact, from one particular (methodological) viewpoint, humanistic existentialism is closer to environmentalism than to phenomenology, its fellow humanistic theory. Both existentialism and phenomenology agree on most ontological points; the primacy of the self, the existence and the necessity of subjective knowledge, and subjectivity being at least as important as objectivity. The divergence comes about concerning the a priori versus a posteriori nature of humanity. It is the ancient question of essence or existence. As previously noted, most humanistic theories accept the notion that essence has preeminence. This essence is that which makes things as they are. It determines the particular characteristics and properties of things. Existentialists, in a tangential fashion, side with environmentalists on this issue and deny that essence is primary or that it precedes existence. They claim that the notion of any ultimate reality derived from an essentialistic self is, by and large, unknowable. Human nature does not come from an a priori essence that makes humanity what it is. Humans are simply what they think and what they do, and that is a province of experience rather than essence. The existentialists not only differ with the phenomenologists, but, in their definition of experience, they also differ from the environmentalists. Perhaps the differences in the three positions concerning existence and essence could best be illustrated by paraphrasing Descartes. His famous statement "I am" came from the Latin word *exsisto*—I exist. In the Latin, this word is derived from "*ex*" and "*sistere*," meaning literally to stand out or to become. The existentialists use Descartes' "I am" very literally to mean I am becoming what I will be as a result of my choices and my experiences. The environmentalist interpretation of Descartes' "I am" might well be, I am becoming what my experiences make me become. The phenomenological rendering of Descartes' "I am" is, I am becoming who I *am* and who it is my nature to become (Misiak & Sexton, 1973).

Epistemology

> All cognitive processes—perception, memory, intuition, inference, and practice—are subject to error, singly and combined. That is why the scope, validity, and nature of knowledge have been problems since the earliest beginnings of philosophy. (Krikorian & Edel, 1959, p. 85)

"In counseling there is universal agreement that some kind of knowledge is communicated" (Barclay, 1971, p. 15). This makes counseling subject to the same epistemological errors that have plagued philosophy, indeed, have plagued mankind from the beginnings of rational thought. Counseling, like any other field, has had to address itself to those questions concerned with knowledge—how it can be attained and what is its nature—before specific psychotherapeutical strategies are evolved. The divergences noted in particular counseling theories come about because the different positions supply different answers to the problems of epistemology. Once again counseling's humanistic positions respond epistemologically with answers generally characterized by those arguments generated in the defense of metaphysics, with, of course, environmentalism adopting many points of its epistemology from the antimetaphysical stance.

Environmental epistemology, in large measure, stems from the ontological position taken by the movement. The key relationship between an environmental theory of "being" and a theory of "knowing" is as follows: when reality is limited to those externally defined phenomena which are visible in a world of experimental manipulation and statistical inference, it greatly affects acceptable theories of knowledge. A reality circumscribed by external phenomena insures that knowledge will be the sole property of scientific fact or scientific principle (Barclay, 1971). If an ontology such as the one adopted by environmentalism were to come to any epistemological position other than the one stated above, it would be violating philosophy's most simple and yet most profound rule, the rule of contradiction. An ontology that recognizes only externally defined phenomena insures that its system of knowing will be sensory—the senses being the only way to perceive externally defined phenomena—and totally attuned to the observational motif described in the scientific method (hypothetico-deductive method). Knowledge thus becomes identified with the products of science. Knowledge is seen as problem-solving skills centered on experience. The environmentalists, as part of their logical positivist heritage, have adopted their methodological canons directly from the principle that the products of science exist as the only knowledge that people are capable of attaining. This idea leads to the logical conclusion that the scientific method is the supreme criterion of philosophic clarity and, in turn, of counseling clarity. Skinner (1976) argued that science is a kind of group consciousness held together by state rules, and laws. The knowledge generated by science provides rules for action and furthers "human behavior in the interest of the human condition" (Skinner, 1976, p. 154). Skinner stated that the beginning advancements of modern science correctly saw this relationship between knowledge and utility and appropriately carried it forward. Reduced logically, the environmental position states: Knowledge is a product of science; science produces utilitarian products; therefore, it follows that knowledge must be scientifically utilitarian.

This line of reasoning can be traced back to the major philosophic movement that champions the place of action and experience in epistemological clarity. This movement is pragmatism. Of all great philosophic movements, none has exerted quite the influence on western society as has pragmatism. This is equally true in the case of western psychology. Environmentalism has drawn heavily on a highly pragmatic theory of knowing. The rise and general acceptance of environmentalism in the psychology of western society coincides with the overall dominance of pragmatism in all parts of western society. As pragmatism gained in stature and acceptance, thanks largely to the contributions of John Dewey, Charles Sanders Peirce, William James, and Auguste Comte, it served as the foundation of many of environmentalism's chief epistemological beliefs. Since pragmatism is primarily a theory of knowledge, it naturally made its greatest contribution to environmentalism in the area of epistemology.

A major pragmatic belief adopted by environmentalism is the idea that experience is the final authority, the real test of all things (Butler, 1951). Hypotheses tested by experience constitute the nearest approach to knowledge that can be attained. "In order to determine the meaning of an idea, it must be put into practice; the consequences which follow constitute the meaning of the idea" (Butler, 1951, p. 443). In the book *Beyond Counseling and Therapy*, Carkhuff and Berenson (1967) noted this pragmatic trend in environmental counseling. "They [environmentalists] use what works and change [experimental procedures] to suit what they perceive the client's needs to be" (p. 92). This adequately exemplifies the similarity between the pragmatic and environmental conception of truth (as was pointed out earlier, conceptions of the nature of truth play a dominant role in epistemological questions). Both positions accept the empirical nature of truth and clearly state that truth, from this frame of reference, is always based on sense-perceptual experience (Butler, 1951). The facts themselves are neither the truth nor the core of knowledge . Rather, it is the pattern for organizing facts which is important. Seen in this manner, truth becomes the successful organization of facts. The pattern for organizing facts that forms the core of knowledge is a hypothesis which works successfully. This successful hypothesis is the key to knowledge, not because it represents some fundamental, absolute principle that can be applied to any situation. Nor is it the key simply because it is a way of acting which brings a needed result. This idea of knowledge based on utility seems much more valuable to the environmentalist than any a priori generalization geared toward absolute truth or ultimate meanings.

The knowledge we have is primarily an affair of acting, doing, and living. "And as such it is not knowledge of an unchangeable sort, which is always true; but it is limited, approximate knowledge, always relative to the present unit of experience" (Butler, 1951, p. 449). The experience itself is neither private nor subjective; it is public and objective. These relative and utilitarian epistemological characteristics demand a methodology based on these same principles. The methods adopted by environmentalism seem consistent with the basic environmental beliefs concerning knowledge and truth and also consistent with the principles of the scientific method. The fundamental epistemological method adopted by environmentalism is easily summarized. Because life is an ongoing process characterized by experiential change, obstacles often appear in this process. These obstacles can produce tension and can substantially alter the flow of all subsequent experiences. When confronted by such obstacles, the first task is to observe any and all facts comprising this particular unit of experience. The collection and analysis of the data surrounding these observed facts will tend to fall into a pattern or perhaps many alternative patterns. These suggested patterns become the hypotheses on which to act. The final step is to test or act upon the suggested hypotheses. The correctness or truth of the method depends solely on the consequences elicited when the hypotheses are acted upon. If, after an hypothesis has been tested, the obstacle still remains, the hypothesis in question is discarded as unsuccessful and another hypothesis is selected. This process continues until an hypothesis is tested which successfully removes the obstacle (Butler, 1951). When the action taken satisfies the demands of the present unit of experience and makes it again flow smoothly and unimpeded by the original obstacle, then the truth for this particular, relative unit of experience has been ascertained. Success, truth, and knowledge is determined by what "works" in a given unit of experience. This method yields knowledge in the limited sense of establishing a particular way of acting which is acceptable to a particular unit of experience. This relative knowledge is said to have value because something is done which causes change and brings a needed result (Butler, 1951). "The ultimate test of truth is whether or not it works. To the degree that a solution solves a problem in the real world of experience, it may be said to be true" (Barclay, 1968, p. 24).

The fact that environmentalism leans heavily on an epistemology dedicated to finding out what works in the real world of experience justifies its label as a problem solving theory. The emphasis is not placed on the subject but rather on the object of knowledge. A problem is identified; ways and means of dealing with this problem are devised; action is then undertaken to solve the problem. In each of these problem solving steps the emphasis is directed away from any understanding of self, and, instead, all emphasis is placed on the objective procedure of environmental adjustment. Nothing overt is done to the subject of the problem solving method. Instead, only the objective realm is considered. The basic assumption for this line of thought is that, by altering a subject's environment, one indirectly will alter the subject since the subject is thought to be a product of the environment. This premise is largely based on the correspondence assumption or, as it is often called, the correspondence theory of truth. "This assumption holds that the subjective world of individual experience can be translated or can correspond to the objective world of reality" (Barclay, 1968, p. 15). If changes can be made in the observable, verifiable, and objective realm of an externally defined environment, then corresponding changes should take place in the internal subjective realm, if indeed such a realm exists. In other words, if objective environmental alterations successfully eliminate a stated problem, then it can be assumed that subjective, internal changes have also taken place. The emphasis is placed on the objective realm because that dimension is observable and verifiable through the senses. One can measure both the changes and the effects of objective manipulation. One can also replicate the procedures in similar cases.

This empirical thread of replicability, observability, and verifiability is evident not only in environmentalism but throughout the entire history of antimetaphysical thought. The belief that empiricism is the only method by which humans can know is fundamental to the position. Simply stated, "empiricism is the belief that the senses teach us all that we know, and they are the only sources of knowledge" (Hocutt, 1980, p. 59). In this area, the environmentalists accent the idea of John

Locke who stated that all knowledge is founded on experience and ultimately derives from experience. "There are no innate ideas, no ideas apart from those experientially derived though the senses" (Gould, 1975, pp. 223–224). Questions about knowledge do not start with an absolute truth waiting to be contemplated or "found." Rather such questions start with a problem presented in experience. If no problems were to arise, then there would be no necessity to even ask questions about knowledge. The existence of any subjective doubt naturally implies that the objective experiential situation contains a problem. To solve the problem one must experiment and physically alter the indeterminate situation (the problem) in such a way as to make it more determinate.

> Hence, knowing is necessarily operational, not just beholding. The inception and verification of knowledge cannot be purely mental. The inquirer must do something to the external situation to see what happens by way of consequences. (John Dewey, 1916, pp. 321–322)

The only proper way to evaluate these consequences is to verify them through the use of the senses.

In this method, acquiring knowledge is incidental to solving a known problem. Learning then is an intimate transaction between a learner or knower and the environment and it always takes place in a specific environmental context.

> Knowledge works outward from individual experience in specific contexts to more general [but not ultimate concepts] which, to remain knowledge, must be continuously tested by subsequent experience. (Brubacher, 1965, p. 123)

Concepts that change or are qualified by subsequent experience become false in that particular context. For a concept to maintain its status as knowledge, it must undergo further experiential testing. If this testing is not forthcoming, the concept becomes mere information on hand rather than knowledge. It is a key environmental contention that as knowledge is reconstructed in the light of experientially testing consequences, it is also probable that a reconstruction of the knower (as well as the known) also occurs. By the same token, it is possible for the whole system to change both its methods and its principles. This process depends entirely on sensory interpretation and on the usefulness of the methods and principles used in making indeterminate situations more determinate (Brubacher, 1965). Truth, seen in this light, is the opinion that is fated to be ultimately agreed upon by scientific investigation, and the experimental or scientific method is the only proper manner to attain those beliefs that will ultimately be accepted by the scientific community (C. S. Peirce, 1955). William James in *The Meaning of Truth* (1909) echoed this idea of truth by stating that the truth is merely what is expedient in our way of thinking, just as notions of right are what are expedient in our way of behaving. John Dewey (1943) summarized this position by saying that truth is a mutable concept. The truth is dependent "on the cultural environment as having [a] pervasive influence on forming the ideas, beliefs, and intellectual attitudes [including truth] of individuals" (White, 1943, p. 58). There is no inquiry into truth itself. Rather, all inquiry is initiated by conditions of doubt, and inquiry ends, not in the establishment of truth, but in the establishment of conditions in which doubt is no longer needed or felt. This is the major goal toward which environmental counseling is directed. The environmental quest is not directed toward any final, abstract meaning for truth. Environmentalists see their proper task as the restructuring of a particular environmental experience in order to ameliorate a given problem of that particular experience. The question in their eyes is not what is truth? The proper question to ask is what can we do to solve a particular problem? For example, they feel that it is absurd to deal with abstractions such as truth and being when they are treating a subject whose problem is an overwhelming fear of heights. In this particular situation all energies should be directed toward finding out what to do to "solve" the specific problem. This problem, in its simplest form, is an obsessive fear of heights, not a philosophical discussion of truth. Success in this problem is not discovering the truth. Rather, success is treating a symptom in order to make the subject unafraid of heights. If this can be accomplished, if this particular problem can be solved, then the nature of truth makes no difference and efforts in this abstract direction are actually harmful because they absorb time that could better be directed toward solving an actual problem.

A final point of environmental epistemology has to do with the ancient philosophic question, how do we learn? This question is somewhat different from the question, what is knowledge and truth? It is also different from the question, how can one test for knowledge and truth? This question involves the actual procedure through which humans learn. Environmentalists have consistently answered the how do we learn question in terms of conditioning. The concept of conditioning makes it easy to replace higher mental processes (governed by a unique self) by forming learning principles based on observable, elementary stimulus-response combinations. Even as early as the opening of this century, Watson (1916) was willing to put all epistemological problems in terms of conditioning. This emphasis continues to be a dominant thread in modern environmental thought. For example, Skinner is considered a most influential spokesman for modern environmentalism and, as with Watson, conditioning principles lie at the heart of his beliefs. (It should perhaps be noted that the term conditioning is not interpreted exactly the same by everyone. Watson saw it in terms of the Russian reflexology experiments of his day [classical conditioning], specifically in terms of Pavlovian conditioned reflexes. But conditioning to Skinner carries the connotation of operant conditioning; the idea of governing behavior through positive reinforcement techniques. Thus conditioning carries subtle shades of differing definitions for various environmentalists). Skinner (ed. Wann, 1964) noted that conditioning principles are objective and verifiable and if embraced would lead to an acceptable empirical epistemology. The process of "knowing" is nothing more than an organism "reacting discriminatively to the world around it under certain contingencies of reinforcement" (Skinner, ed. Wann, 1964, p. 85). Skinner (1964) often stated the belief that the idea of repetitive conditioning was the proper answer to the question, how do we learn? His answer is typical of the environmental position, and it leaves no room for anything which could be considered "mental" in epistemological processes.

Environmentalists point to objective studies showing the success rate of an epistemology devoted mainly to conditioning techniques. "On the whole, they [the clinical studies] support the proposition that counter-conditioning is the mechanism by which behavior modification works" (Goldstein, ed. Corsini, 1973, p. 212). This epistemology is very deterministic in that it accepts the idea that every behavior is completely determined by antecedent factors (Goldstein, ed. Corsini, 1973). By engaging in conditioning techniques that seek to control or modify the antecedent factors that are responsible for a certain behavior, one could "determine" a chosen consequence. "These consequences or behaviors are simply responses to stimulation, and the pattern of the responses is the result of learning" (Goldstein, ed. Corsini, 1973, p. 219). The goal of the environmentalist is to reverse unadaptive learning and furnish proper learning experiences where appropriate responses have not been previously exhibited. This is accomplished in a framework of the canons of the scientific method, basic stimulus-response methodology, and the necessary conditioning techniques. Many supporters of environmentalism believe that these scientific epistemological standards account for both the modern acceptance and popularity of this position. Many within the movement would agree that perhaps

> the largest contribution of behavior therapy [environmentalism] may prove to be the introduction of the scientific method to the field of psychotherapy, thus opening the way for development of the field from a philosophical trade union to one in which demonstrable results become the "sine qua non" for acceptance. (Goldstein, ed. Corsini, 1973, p. 217)

In his book *Theory and Practice of Counseling Psychotherapy*, Corey (1977) provided an excellent summary of the epistemological position of environmentalism. The position is well grounded in a learning theory based on conditioning and is concerned not with understanding but with bringing about a needed behavior change. The emphasis is on operationally defined, observable, verifiable, and measurable behavior. Environmentalists feel that carefully controlled experiments will eventually yield the laws that govern behavior, but these experiments must be limited to observable data. There is also the important belief that humans are determined by socio-cultural environments and through this environmental conditioning all behavior, even maladaptive behavior, is learned. Environmentalism is an inductive approach based on experiments and applying the scientific method to the therapeutic process. In this process the therapist functions in a position of authority as a teacher. The treatment concentrates on overt, specific behavior and spells out treatment goals, specific methods, and an objective, measurable form of assessment (behavior change) (Corey, 1977).

As with humanistic concepts of ontology, humanist epistemology is largely based on Descartes' famous dictum about knowledge; the only thing man can know for sure is that precisely at a given point in time he is experiencing a stream of thoughts and feelings. All processes of rationality are based on this precept. The world of science does indeed play a part in our outer reality, but it is a small part because how one relates to the outer world (science, sensation, phenomena) is partially determined by one's own personal psychic structure and by an interaction of past and present experiences. A human mind is not a mere biological adaptation. It possesses an a priori structure of its own. A mind of this type can grasp new concepts and create new facts and ideas. The key attribute of this mind is a notion of the innate power that is usually termed intuition. This is the creative, analytic, and synthetic potential that is an a priori given and is innately present in all human cognitive structure. This apprehension of the innate principles of ontology and epistemology is preconscious and centers on human experience as an experience that is the product of both sensory input and innate structural formation (Barclay, 1971).

> This human experience is valued as apodictically certain, that is, immediate and self-evident. This kind of experience, although not susceptible to the canons of external phenomena in the scientific sense of physics, is, nonetheless valued highly in the hierarchy of certitude. (Barclay, 1971, p. 307)

Husserl (cited in Spiegelberg, 1960) called these concepts a transcendental idealism and noted that, in opposition to environmentalism, it is concerned with the subjective grounds of human experience, the structure of consciousness, and those a priori contentions that constitute the subjective grounds of experience. Spiegelberg (1960) stated that this direct use of intuition could properly serve as the final test for all philosophical knowledge (and, because philosophical knowledge lies at the base of all other forms of knowledge, this intuition conversely is seen as the final test for all knowledge). These notions of humanist epistemology are constructed in a philosophic framework and

> represent not only intellectual analysis and recomposition of scientific data but also the creation of feeling and will of mind which approaches these sensory and perceptual data with definite needs and requirements. (Kulpe, 1897, p. 22)

The humanist position claims that it proposes a broader role for counseling than environmental theories that still hold tightly to the propositions of logical positivism (even after most of the propositions of logical positivism have long been discredited). Humanists complain that environmental concepts fail because they are totally restricted to the products of the scientific method. They use this method also, but they are more concerned with an epistemology which considers human perception and makes inquiry about the structure of human consciousness.

In his analysis of epistemology, Kant (cited in Hoernle, 1927) stated that pure sensation was a process of chaos in which all kinds of sensory stimulation are passively received by the mind. This sensory chaos attains order through two categories of perception, space and time. Conceptual thinking is achieved through a rational categorization of sensory input by a priori mental structures. Though it is the sensory data which may impress on the mind, it is the mind itself that invests that experiential sensory data with meaning. Humanists do not reject the importance of this sensory input nor do they reject the importance of objective scientific precepts in building epistemological concepts. Humanists differ because they believe that valid knowledge can be achieved through other means than scientific deduction.

Edmund Husserl (cited by Schmitt, 1967) spent much of his career arguing for the validity of nonempirical forms of knowledge. Husserl felt that psychology deals with facts and therefore its statements can be said to be empirical. But still it has yet to produce precise scientific laws and often its generalizations are vague. The rules of logic are precise; thus, psychological laws based purely on empiricism cannot be identical to logical laws, nor can such generalizations be premises from which logical laws can be derived. Empirical statements can only be probable. There is always a very real possibility that future evidence will prove them false. (As, for example, many of Einstein's discoveries proved Newtonian "laws" false.) Logical truths, though, are necessary truths. Empirical arguments rest on the principles of deduction and are derived from a number of individual cases.

> Thus, where there is a conflict between a logical principle and an empirical generalization, the logical principle will always be victorious because necessary truth is not to be refuted by a probable statement and also because logical truth cannot be shown to be false by a deductive generalization. (Husserl, cited by Schmitt, 1967, p. 137)

The key goal of an empirical generalization is to produce causal laws. Logical principles do not produce such laws nor are they the product of such causal laws. It was Husserl's contention that the principles and conclusions of an argument are not related to cause and effect relationships. "The truth of a conclusion is not the effect of the truth of the premises. Causal relations hold between events, and events happen at a definite time and in a definite place" (Husserl, cited by Schmitt, 1967, p. 137). But the premise of an argument does not just "happen" in a specific time or place, nor does the conclusion. Premises and conclusions are either true or false principles, not experiential events. In a valid argument the truth of a conclusion "follows" from the premises; it is not the "effect" of events called premises. Any empirical law implies a matter of fact; logical rules do not. All empirical laws are derived from the observation of particulars. The truth of the empirical law thus depends on the situation of the particular and the powers (not always infallible) of the observer. Thus the existence of these particulars can only be inferred from the "truth" of the empirical law. "Leibnitz phrased this better by saying that empirical laws are true [probably] for this actual world; logical laws are true for all possible worlds" (Husserl, cited by Schmitt, 1967, p. 137).

To one espousing the humanist position, these arguments are not simply mental exercises. The arguments provide a logical, rational base to accept forms of knowledge over and above empirical knowledge. The arguments state that logical and empirical laws differ in kind and that logical statements are precise, necessarily true, and not derived deductively from particulars. Such statements produce logical rules, not causal laws, and they are not simple matters of fact to be studied through the senses. These considerations are compared to empirical statements which are vague, probably, but not necessarily, true, and are the products of deductive generalizations. These statements produce causal laws and interpretations based solely on matters of facts derived through the senses. These humanistic arguments are important because they provide a logical base for an epistemology that is not the sole result of science and empirical laws. Phenomenology, Rogers' client centered theories, gestalt theories, existentialism, and all other counseling "third forces" are founded on the position established in the above arguments that truth and knowledge are not totally dependent on empirical sensate observation. Thus, humanist epistemology makes room for intuition, a priori essences, and reflective thinking. This reflective mode of thought does not concentrate only on facts or specific actions. This type of reflection concentrates on examples, on the necessary conditions for an object's being an example of a certain kind of thing. This reflection involves intuition and sincere questioning. Objective knowledge is always only a shadow of that ultimate knowledge which lies at the base of reality. Since this ultimate reality is believed by humanists to be a world of ideas, not senses, they feel that a subjective, reflective, and intuitive approach founded on a framework of logic is the proper way to know this ultimate reality. Knowledge may indeed be based on experience, but it is the experience of perception that brings knowledge, not the experience of sensation as claimed by John Locke and other empiricists. The act of perception shapes sensory representation (Barclay, 1968). Knowledge is therefore not a simple passive image brought about by quantitative sensory intensity. Rather, it will be more readily conceived when it does not concentrate exclusively on either the objects of experience or on the subject of experience, but on the point of contact where being and consciousness meet (Edi, cited in Thevenaz, 1962). It is the active structuring of the mind itself. External phenomena supply the content of the experience, but it is the unique, perceptually subjective self that invests the experience with individual meaning (Barclay, 1968).

All knowledge has to be mediated through the process of perception and therefore any image of external reality is not only determined by the nature of the environmental transmission but also by the a priori structure of the receiver. This structure and subject of perception is found in humanity, and this human nature filters all sensory representation in accordance with a learned reservoir of experience and also in accordance with basic structure of consciousness. Thus, the meaning of any act and the interpretation of any phenomena are arrived at through both environmental stimuli and the structure of the perceiving apparatus (Barclay, 1968). This epistemology is concerned with and related to the subject of knowledge, i.e., the individual self, and not merely the object of knowledge, i.e., sensory received phenomena.

The process of incorporating this epistemological scheme into a counseling strategy is actually quite simple. The process is highly verbalized, and this verbalization is usually of a noncognitive, non-empirical nature. The counselor does not operate with any degree of omnipotence or leadership. They, counselor and client, are simply involved together in a fairly equal relationship. This counselor involvement rather than leadership helps the client to form useful insights and deeper degrees of self-understanding. These steps, if practiced as a consequence of dialogue in a nonthreatening, permissive environment, will lead the client to discovery and knowledge of that unique self that ontologically lies at the heart of the humanist position. This self is able to perceive and understand the truth, not because it corresponds with observed facts, but because truth is a coherent, decipherable quality when measured in terms of its consistency with other truths. It is not simply a product of science, but rather it is the apprehension of truth through the structure of the conscious mind of a unique self. Seen in this fashion truth is not a product of the deductive approach. "It will get us nowhere to pare away the qualities of an object one by one, assuming that eventually we will get at the thing itself" (Butler, 1966, p. 65). There is no benefit in dealing with phenomena or experience in isolation from the rest of existence or from our own selves.

> Every object, every part of experience, is what it is just because of its relation to the whole. True knowledge... can only be achieved by seeing them in their relations to the whole (Butler, 1966, p. 65).

This idea of consistency with other truths and relatedness is very important in humanistic counseling because self-understanding is a key to this position. Since all individuals are best understood in relation to other individuals, it seems probable that self-knowledge (a key goal of humanism) is achieved by learning to know others. "Our fellow is the medium in which we see the nature and meaning of our own mind reflected" (Creighton, ed. Robinson, 1929, p. 146). Thus, in humanistic counseling thought the individual can only be understood and can only understand oneself in terms of a relation to other selves.

As with humanistic ontology, it should perhaps be noted that there are also inconsistencies in humanist epistemology, and also as with ontology this inconsistency is caused by existentialism. As a prominent member of humanistic thought, existentialism again agrees with most epistemological canons of the position: the ascendance of the subjective over the objective, the importance of being able to create one's own experiences through the application of free choice, and the importance of insight and intuitive and reflective thought. The key epistemological inconsistency brought about by existentialism is basically the same as the previously discussed ontological inconsistency. Again, it is the question of essence versus existence. Existentialism get much of its epistemological beliefs from philosophers such as Soren Kierkegaard (cited in Mullen, 1981). These thinkers rejected the notion of essence, universals, and a priori structures. In their interpretation, existentialism is not interested in the why of behavior, it is interested only in the fact of behavior. Sartre (1947) translated this as meaning that human beings do not possess a priori knowledge or being but are rather products of what they will themselves to be and also their experiences. May, Angel, and Ellenberger (1958) felt that the emphasis should be placed on the transitory, immediate, self-evident nature of life experiences in which questions of essential structure and studies of consciousness are to be bypassed in favor of an examination of the unique characteristics of experience. Knowledge is concerned only with matters of existence and the here and now of on-going daily experience. To the existentialist all knowledge is a posteriori and is thus based on experience and observation while other humanistic epistemological schemes believe in an a priori structure of knowledge, with principles that are self-evident and, when once understood, are recognized as true and do not require proof through observation, experience, or experiment (Butler, 1951).

In the place of an essential a priori structure for knowledge, existentialism favors a simple theory of epistemology based on the prospect of nonbeing. It is this ever present knowledge of the imminence of nonbeing that is the one absolute that all men share (Barclay, 1971). To the existentialist all other knowledge is reduced to insignificance in the face of this awareness of nonbeing. Essence is simply not a believable or important term. How a person lives determines his essence. It is a product of experience, not an innate a priori structure. This humanistic inconsistency of the relative merits of essence and existence is present throughout the entire philosophical structure of the movement. It will present itself again in the discussion of humanistic values.

Axiology

Axiology is a philosophical term denoting a general theory of value. It is concerned with the nature of values, the different kinds of value, and a consideration of specific values that are worthy of possession (Butler, 1951). As with the other major philosophical foundations of counseling, there is again a marked difference in environmental and humanistic systems of value. Also, these differences once again find their genesis in the philosophic debate (metaphysics versus antimetaphysics) examined earlier. Almost all of the following examples of environmental axiology consistently reflect the arguments used by antimetaphysicians to validate their position. Humanist axiology is founded on concepts established in metaphysical precepts, and as such it again represents an antithetical position toward most environmental pronouncements concerning value.

In its most generalized form, environmental values in counseling represent a rough combination of hedonism and utilitarianism. It is hedonistic because one of its key goals is to ameliorate a problem and return an individual to a state of contentment. It is utilitarian because, even though it deals with individuals, it has, as its basic frame of reference, society as a whole. It attempts, through conditioning techniques, to achieve the greatest happiness for the greatest number in a society. Skinner's book *Walden II* (1948) is an excellent example of this. It is a moralistic fable designed to show how scientific conditioning techniques, judiciously applied to every individual. could create a better and more worthwhile society. It is a saga which states that morals and values are learned behaviors, and therefore society would benefit if it espoused a better way to teach and instruct its individual members in proper moral behavior and in the selection of worthwhile values. Skinner clearly stated that he believed that conditioning techniques exist as the best way to accomplish this societal utilitarianism. In *Science and Human Behavior* Skinner (1953) devoted a separate chapter to this idea of purposefully engendering acceptable morals and values in the individual participants of a society. He claimed that it was "possible to change the social environment deliberately so that the human product will meet more acceptable specifications" (Skinner, 1953, p. 427).

Seen environmentally, values and morals are extensions of the ontological and epistemological principles already discussed. Humans are biological products of their environment, and they learn through sense impressions generated through the environment and through simple stimulus-response conditioning techniques. Values are no different from any other behavior, and, be they adaptive or nonadaptive, they are learned. The environment can be modified to some extent to produce (condition) the "right" behavior in any relative time reference.

Because science plays such a key role in every theory of environmental epistemology, it is also seen as a key to values, since values and morals are simply extensions of learned behavior. Thus science, if used properly, should be a social pursuit and should be applied cooperatively to the study of all of humanity's problems in order to enhance the common good (Butler, 1951). Science is also important to this axiology because of its insistence on observable experimentation. Environmentalists claim that there is nothing absolute or ultimate in the realm of values. Morals, values, and ethical behaviors are properly attributed to environmental contingencies (cultural and environmental reinforcers), and this leaves no room for absolute considerations. This yields a kind of relativism in which "good" is whatever a particular society decides to call good (Skinner, 1976). An individual is not moral because he behaves morally nor does he behave morally because he is moral. "He behaves morally and we call him moral because he lives in a particular kind of environment" (Skinner 1976, p. 213). There is "no reason to suppose that any cultural practice is always right or wrong according to some principle or value, regardless of the circumstance" (Skinner, 1953, p. 436). Science helps in the development and assessment of the relative values of a society. It aids humanity in deciding between alternative courses of action. These alternative courses can never be either absolutely right or wrong. They are merely different courses of action. By making past consequences effective in determining future conduct, science aids us in our choice of these alternative courses of action.

> Although no one course of action may be exclusively dictated by scientific experience, the existence of a scientific parallel, no matter how sketchy, will make it somewhat more likely that the more profitable of two courses will be taken. (Skinner, 1953, p. 436)

The formalized experience of science and the practical experience of an individual involved in a specific set of circumstances provide humankind's best hope for forming values and moral judgments. Skinner (1953) stated that any value not formed through environmental contingencies, the formalized experience of science, and the practical experience of an individual is then merely formed as a product of pure guesswork. "Science does not eliminate guessing, but by scientifically narrowing the field of alternative courses of action, it helps us to guess more effectively" (Skinner, 1953, p. 436).

Environmentalism rejects the notion of purposeful behavior. Values and morals are not selected on any basis of right and wrong. Rather, moralistic behavior is like every other piece of human behavior in that it is believed to be a "function of some condition that is describable in physical terms" (Malcolm, ed. Wann, 1964, p. 142). Man does not possess any innate structure, as Kant argued, that leads to a sense of morality. Skinner (ed. Wann, 1964) stated quite clearly his belief in the impossibility of moral behavior as a result of inner direction. Morality is just one of the resulting products one achieves by reinforcing a particular action. This thought lies at the heart of environmental axiology.

Malcolm (ed. Wann, 1964) traced the axiological base of environmental thought back to Rudolf Carnap's doctrine of "physicalism." This doctrine states that psychological sentences may be formulated in physical language. These sentences describe physical occurrences, namely the physical behavior, including so-called moral behavior, of all humanity. The foundation for this thesis is the verification principle. Thus, the meaning of a statement or a behavior is its method of verification, or as Carnap (1959) put it, a sentence or a behavior says no more than what is testable about it. In this interpretation, a statement made about another person, that this person is moral or good, means no more than that one observes that person to be behaving in a particular way and that the person will measurably respond in a specific fashion to certain stimuli, and that physically the central nervous system is in a particular state of functioning (Carnap, 1959). In this position, it is ridiculous to claim that over and above these observable physical facts there exists some inner state of morality which is different from the actual or potential behavior and the physiological state of the organism. The belief in so-called inner directed actions, i.e., motivations of right and wrong, over and above the physical facts cannot stand because it claims the existence of something which is impossible to verify. Without that verification, one is again indulging in pure guesswork (Malcolm, ed. Wann, 1964). All behavior, including moral behavior, must be examined in this manner and not in terms of inner, goal-directed behavior or purposeful action. In every case, if examined closely, the terms goal and purpose are reducible to statements about operant conditioning, and they take their place in the framework of a natural science. Morality and values are simply the results of consequences that have followed similar behaviors in the past.

Most environmentalists agree that any absolute base for value is in error. The so-called absolute values identified in past societies were, upon investigations, merely agreements within that society. The great religious texts of the past were not examples of any absolute valuation, even though most people under the influence of these texts erroneously considered them to be absolutes. In point of fact, these religious texts were simply examples of the deliberate construction of a social environment. The rules were agreed upon by a majority of a particular society's membership and were enforced, not on principles of right and wrong, but through reinforcement techniques; either punishment or positive reward as meted out by the group or religious agency selected by that particular society. Skinner (1953) maintained that the "Ten Commandments" were perfect examples of the idea whereby a majority of a society agreed to a codification of rules and enforced those rules through both positive and negative conditioning techniques. The members learned their morality as a result of the consequences generated by any particular act.

In an explanation for value such as this, it can easily be seen that notions of good and evil cannot be apprehended outside the context of a given social setting. The problem of what should one do, i.e., what is the proper behavior, depends solely on what ends one has in mind and what ends an individual's society has in view. Environmentalists claim that this has always been the human way of establishing morality, but by approaching it in such an unscientific manner, historically, humanity has not been very successful in its dealings with questions of morality. It is a principal contention of environmental axiology that a particular society's morality is best served when that morality is founded on verifiable scientific postulates. In this manner, a society would benefit because its morality would be based on the best scientific insights available. This reliance on a society's best scientific endeavor constitutes the only reliable guide to human conduct, both individual and social. In such a society as that recommended by environmentalists, the highest value is that which is based on scientific fact. "When the facts are extended to social behavior, it holds that science should be able to provide the answers to what constitutes ethical and moral human behavior" (Barclay, 1971, p. 399).

Environmental thought insists that this method of "creating" values is of much more worth than depending on concepts of absolute value. By concentrating on absolutes, one is forced to give up thinking about value because absolutes are not subject to question or inquiry. They simply exist and must be obeyed. This is a nonsensical way to approach moral behavior to the environmentalist. Morality is better considered and understood as a function of a certain circumstance and a consideration of whatever arrangements that could be effected to bring about an improvement in that circumstance. This environmental position on axiology logically follows from the ontological and epistemological stances adopted by the movement. With the environmental theory of being and knowledge examined earlier, it would be logically impossible for the movement to accept a theory of value contrary to that outlined in this section.

As with the case of environmentalism, humanistic axiology logically follows from the ontological and epistemological positions adopted by the movement. The judgement of what is good or what is right or wrong is determined from what can be known about the nature of the ultimate and universal principles or ground of human experience, as reflected in self-consciousness. These moral judgements are largely founded on the intuition of certain moral insights that are revealed from within the structure of the mind, the unique personal self, in basically the same manner as cognitive awareness (Barclay, 1971). The highest good, the "summon bonum", is the aim or objective of living which is above all other ends. In absolutist philosophies, such as those drawn upon by humanism, this aim is toward the ultimate end, which by its very nature cannot be a means to another end. The absolutist philosophy adopted by humanism is the quest for the perfect. The ultimate of highest good is the perfection for the self, or self-realization. For humanism, this idea carries a social corollary. Perfection is expanded from an individual to include a social order as the ultimate objective of society (Butler, 1951).

In large part, the humanistic theory of value is directly traceable to the works of Immanuel Kant. Clifford Barrett (1935) stated that Kant "developed the most important expression of perfectionism yet given in the modern world" (p. 330). The selection of values which tend toward the perfect are not apprehended strictly as a product of our emotions or feelings. Rather, these particular values "are realities which have existence themselves and are rooted in the very structure of the cosmos" (Butler, 1951, p. 207). Humanity is aware of these ultimate values because the "being" of an individual self is ultimately intertwined with this cosmos. Kant (cited in Butler, 1951) contended that a human being is more than a "thing" or a biological organism. They have minds, personalities, souls, and unique selves and thus have potentialities far higher in quality and ultimate worth than other forms of existence. Kant's chief moral point was that a person is a unique, conscious self and therefore exists as an "end" and was never meant to be a "means" to an end. When parts of humanity begin to employ other parts of humanity as a means to achieve a cultural, economic, industrial, or military end, it marks the failure of human morality. People are innately ends in themselves, and it represents the highest form of moral perversion to use them as a means to some impersonal objective.

Everyone, according to Kant, carries within themselves, within the structure of their consciousness, an innate imperative to do good. This is as much a part of human nature as sensation, perception, and thought. Through the powers of reason, the innate structure of consciousness reveals that there are moral laws which are absolute and universally binding. If these moral laws are disregarded, all social order would give way to chaos and confusion. These universal moral laws are essential because each person is a unique self. As a self, one can reasonably act only in those ways which one would be willing to grant as a universal practice to all other selves. The evils condemned in the "Ten Commandments" are evil because they violate the above concept and are contrary to respect for others as unique personal selves (Butler, 1951).

The idea that each person is a unique self capable of understanding universal moral laws through reason, logically leads to a concept of an ideal society. "If individuals are persons, and if all individuals control their conduct in harmony with complete respect for other persons, human society will become an ideal society of ends" (Butler, 1951, p. 211). Kant (1938) summarized the moral theories of humanism when he declared that each self should treat all other people as selves, and also for each self to live as though already a member of an ideal society of ends. Morality is not a question of which behavior is reinforced and which extinguished through conditioning techniques. Morality is not based on scientific pragmatism. Humanist morality is part of the innate, a priori structure of consciousness that makes each person a unique self. Through the innate structure and through the intuition of certain moral insights, each self has the opportunity to encounter and incorporate the universal moral laws as a part of a personal self. Ultimately, human beings are then to conduct themselves according to personal maxims of freedom that take into account the necessary respect for other selves as they attempt to move toward the universal laws of morality (Barclay, 1968).

William Hitt (1969) recognized a fundamental characteristic of humanist morality when he compared a so-called behavioral model of humankind to a humanistic model. He noticed that the behaviorist saw value formation in terms of a human passivity governed by external stimuli. The values change as the stimuli are changed. The key concept of the humanist is not just a denial of this process. Humanists, of course, reject this view of human nature, but they also replace this view with one more in concert with the idea that human beings are special. They are not passive receptors but are instead the source of personal acts and personal morality. They are not shaped. They shape themselves because they are free to choose in each situation. The essence of humanity is only in humanity, and it is controlled only by one's own consciousness. Karl Jaspers (cited in Beck, 1963) made this same case. He spoke of the authentic or transcendent self that is beyond the study of empirical methods or procedures. This self is not a stimulus-response product of a particular environment. It is rather the source of all meaning and value in life. This self makes choices that defy severe environmental limitations, and in this defiance it moves toward ultimate meanings.

Even though the personal self is the mechanism through which one interprets value, it is a social setting or a society of other selves that bestows meaning to these values. This belief comes from the idea that a society is not a collection of individuals; it is an entity in which individuals participate. The self cannot grow in isolation. It can realize its selfhood and strive toward its perfection only in relation to a society of other selves. This does not subordinate the individual, and a self is still seen as an end and not a means. But society is seen as an end also, and at the same time an individual progresses toward a meaningful end, that self simultaneously promotes the progress of society to its end also. So, even though the self is unique and individual, it can only find its meaning in a society of other selves. This principle is roughly akin to the existentialist concept in which the self is seen in three parts. The "Umwelt" is that part of the self recognized by the environmentalists; it is the organic or biological self. The "Mitwelt" is a world of interpersonal relationships where the meaning of others in the group is partly determined by one's own relationship to each of them. This relationship carries a sense of responsibility, commitment, and communion. The last stage identified by the existentialists is the "Eigenwelt." This stage is the exact opposite of an environmentalist who sees value in a person only because the self mirrors the group around it, the old idea of being shaped by the environment. The Eigenwelt is that complex territory of personal expressions of deep inner-directed value. The concept of love is an example of such statements of value. Kierkegaard (1954) stated that one remains incapable of love until one "has comprehended the deep secret that also in loving another person one must be sufficient unto himself" (p. 55). This sufficiency unto oneself is the existentialist and humanist concept of the Eigenwelt. One must totally come to an understanding of one's own unique self before an understanding of other selves can take place. Kierkegaard and even Nietzche insisted that one must become a true individual before attempting to contribute to a society's morality or even its existence (Kemp, 1971).

For a humanist, the term value means more than adjustment to one's environment. The meaningfulness of a life is perhaps a better criterion of mental health than the mere absence of physical or psychic pain (Frankl, 1955). This idea of meaningfulness is a concept found only in humanistic theories. It applies to a relation to one's own self and to a relation to that society of which one is an integral part. Meaningfulness is discovered only as one progresses toward a self-realization (perfectionism) and acts as an efficient cause in moving one's society toward this same group realization (perfection).

In its value structure, humanism is very reminiscent of the principle of justice as outlined in Plato's Republic. A society cannot be an end unless it provides a genuine opportunity for each self that composes that society to actively participate in its activities and deliberations. Societies are not, or at least they should not be, blind social processes that occur without regard to its members. They have the power to deliberate, form objectives, and guide social processes. When a society treats its individuals with respect for their innate self-hood and when it is representative, it is at least partially able to become self-conscious about its own existence and move toward its proper end. Humanists state that counseling must consider values in this fashion if it is to aid humanity on either an individual or social level. There is the argument that psychotherapy belongs strictly to the realm of science and is not concerned with value, but in *The Doctor and the Soul,* Frankl (1973) stated the humanist position on this issue very clearly when he said that he believed that "there was no such thing as psychotherapy unconcerned with values, only one that was blind to values" (p. xi).

Once again, it must be noted that a major thrust within humanism, existentialism, differs on one particular axiological point. Existential values are a direct result of the existential conception of knowledge. Although agreeing with most humanist concerns about value, existentialism refuses to accept the idea of an a priori structure to consciousness or an essence that intuits universal or absolute value. Values are created only by one's existence. Experiences and choices form a value structure, not a mystical intuition of innate principles derived from the cosmos. Epistemologically, existentialism acknowledges that all humanity is alone in the universe of experience. This aloneness is a common union to all people, just as is the ever-present threat of nonbeing. This is the only absolute recognized by the existentialist. Death is not relative. Of course, it should be parenthetically recognized that other forms of humanism argue that, by accepting this simple absolute, existentialism totally acknowledges the possibility of other absolutes. Humanity's sense of value must of necessity proceed from this knowledge (Barclay, 1971). Values are formed as a result of choices formed in the face of this knowledge. A person can run away from this absolute bit of knowledge and not live up to the potential to either self or others and face anxiety and guilt as a consequence. Or one can accept this knowledge and put it to constructive use in realizing the finiteness of being and also to constructively use the short time one has to fulfill commitments to fellow beings and to pursue one's own potential self-realization.

God

It seems likely that many, both environmentalists and humanists, will disagree with the following statements and conclusions concerning this final major metaphysical category. The category is included for two reason: In his article "Five Philosophical Issues in Counseling," Arbuckle (1958) identified five important philosophic influences on the make-up of a counselor. One of these influences was the nature of one's religious beliefs and background. This is simply another way of noting the importance of how one sees the nature of God in terms of the influence it exerts within each of us. It is obviously Arbuckle's theory that the way one answers the question, who or what is God, is a major determinant of not only what type counselor one will be but also, more essentially, what type person one will be. If the issue is that important, then it deserves at least a passing investigation. The second reason for the inclusion of this topic is that the philosophic topics already considered, being, knowing, and valuing, either explicitly or implicitly lead one to a certain position regarding the nature of God. A consideration of the ontology, epistemology, and axiology of both environmentalism and humanism logically extends to a consistent philosophical position regarding the nature of God. It must be remembered that this logical extension is not particularly useful when applied to individuals. Obviously there are theistic, agnostic, and atheistic practitioners of both environmentalism and humanism. But considered abstractly and at the most fundamental level possible, each position's adoption of the philosophical assumptions governing being, knowing, and valuing points toward a position on the nature of God that is consistent with their other philosophical assumptions.

An investigation of the philosophic assumptions of environmentalism that logically extends to a stated nature for God will be quite simple and brief. This is because the foundations of environmental thought leave very little room for a God, at least not in the usual meaning of that term. Environmentalism adopts a highly naturalistic stance toward this topic. Viewed logically, this naturalism makes no place for any supernatural nature for God. In this view, god, if indeed there is a god, can only be viewed as part and parcel of the natural world. Certain ideas of pantheism can very obviously be fitted to this conception of god. A pure naturalism defines and limits god completely within the natural order. The physical universe is the only possible universe, and it forms the primary context of human life. This context is human evolution, biological forces and adaptations, psychology, social relations, and institutions. No supernatural entity could exist over and above this context, nor could it exert any influence on humanity within this context. Nothing exists apart from human experience. If a god exists within these naturalistic parameters, he cannot possess any qualities of ultimacy, no ultimate goodness, no omnipotence, and no omnisciency (Butler, 1951). These commodities logically have to be omitted according to environmental theories of being, knowing, and valuing. In this system a god can exist, but he must be a finite god subject to the same restrictions as the rest of the natural, physical universe.

In this system, reality is described in terms of external phenomena, forces, and laws. Beyond this, there is no need to appeal to a subjective "higher court." Humanity and the universe can adequately be dealt with on these terms because these phenomena, forces, and laws can be known through sensory perception; they can be measured and verified. This ontological principle of verification espoused by the logical positivists and drawn upon by environmental psychology logically carries over into a discussion of god. A. J. Ayer (1946) dismissed this topic on both ontological and epistemological grounds. He claimed that the possibility of a god or the possibility of religious knowledge would have to be shown empirically before it could be accepted. God is a metaphysical term and as such it is senseless. "For to say that 'God exists' is to make a metaphysical utterance which cannot be either true or false" (Ayer, 1946, p. 115). No sentence which purports to describe the nature of a transcendent God can possess any literal significance because no circumstance and no hypothesis for an experiment could be created whereby such a transcendent nature could be observed.

> The notion of a person whose essential attributes are nonempirical is not an intelligible notion at all. We may have a word which is used as if it named this "person," but, unless the sentences in which it occurs express propositions which are empirically verifiable, it cannot be said to symbolize anything. (Ayer, 1946, p. 116)

The sentence "God exists" is a perfect example of this nonsymbolic proposition.

Ayer (1946) saw this question of transcendency as the chief source of antagonism between religion and science. He claimed that scientific knowledge answered, in verifiable form, all the questions of a physical world, thus removing one's motive to find religious answers. Many logical positivists believed that "deep down" even religious people agreed with their pronouncements. These men of religion admitted themselves that a knowledge of a supernatural God is nonsense. "If a mystic admits that the object of his vision is something which cannot be described, then he must also admit that he is bound to talk nonsense when he describes it" (Ayer, 1946, p. 118). Just because one has a "religious experience," it in no way implies religious knowledge. The believer may believe this experience to have cognitive content, but unless a person can formulate this "knowledge" into propositions that are empirically verifiable, he/she is at best confusing some sense data and at worst completely deceiving oneself. No act of intuition can reveal a truth unless it can also be verified empirically, and if this were to happen, it would, of course, no longer be intuition, but would be incorporated in the system of physical empirical propositions which constitute science (Ayer, 1946).

This "replacement" of God by science is not only a reflection of the positivist psychological heritage, it is also part of the large legacy that Freud left to psychology. For Freud, a belief in God was made unnecessary by the advent of modern science. Science became, as Freud called it, "our god logos" (cited in Kung, 1978, p. 302). In this idea of science, Freud claimed that he had found the sure support that is lacking for believers in God. Freud influenced psychology not to abandon the concept of faith, but to abandon the idea of faith in a God. Faith itself was still seen by Freud as a viable term when rightly applied to a reasonable object of that faith. For Freud that object was natural science. "We believe that it is possible for scientific work to gain knowledge about the reality of the world, for our science is no illusion" (Freud, cited in Kung, 1978, p. 302). Freud bequeathed to psychology the idea of an illusionary god produced as a quirk of man's psychic structure.

> After the total animal had ceased to serve as a substitute for him, the primal father, at once feared and hated, revered and envied, became the prototype of God himself. The son's rebelliousness and his affection for his father struggled against each other through a constant succession of compromises, which sought on one hand to atone for the act of parricide and on the other to consolidate the advantage it had brought. (Freud, cited in Kung, 1978, p. 280)

God is therefore to be explained psychologically, and his nature is merely a father complex and one's ambivalent reaction to that complex.

The whole of the environmental position is a rejection of all absolutes—including God—except absolute exactness in the natural sciences. The notion of God cannot be approached on the basis of psychic experiences. It can be approached on a basis of physically verifiable events with the language of physics as the universal language of all science. But when approached in this manner the entire concept of god is meaningless because it cannot be verified (Carnap, cited in Kung, 1978). The idea of God cannot be included within this parameter and therefore cannot be thought to be real or meaningful.

Environmentalism's thoughts concerning god and religion are absolutely consistent with the other major philosophical concerns of the movement. The direct influence of scientific naturalism, experimentalism, logical empiricism, pragmatism, and, to a lesser degree, Freudian thought have all contributed to the rejection of a supernatural being having either a general role in shaping the cosmos or a particular role concerning humankind. This does not mean, though, that the position necessarily rejects the entire notion of a god. They say that under certain conditions, limitations, and boundaries a god might exist. But the nature of these prescribed limitations forbids the idea of God as is normally conceived in western theology. Environmental ontology, epistemology, and axiology logically exclude such a view of God. Where being is limited to sensationally derived (observable and measurable) phenomena, and knowing is a product of scientifically testable hypotheses, and valuing is a result of conditioning for the greatest good for the greatest number without any ideas of absolute principles, then the ideas concerning the nature of god are basically limited to those ideas explored earlier in this section.

> Only by a methodic orientation to the natural sciences as a whole and by testing and verifying all statements empirically is it possible to make any decisive progress... and finally inaugurate a new, fully rational epoch. That alone, therefore, can be regarded as real and meaningful which gives expression to a fact, which is accessible to direct observation and can be tested by experiments. (Kung, 1978, pp. 98–99)

These foundational environmental beliefs leave very little room, at least at the level of basic assumptions, for an ultimate God, either philosophically or in counseling.

As would be expected from the previous examination of ontology, epistemology, and axiology, the idea of God in humanistic doctrines differs radically from environmentalism. Before proceeding to a specific discussion of humanism's view of God, it would perhaps be advisable to offer a brief explanation of humanism as the word is used in this study. In modern usage, the term humanism often appears as "secular humanism" and is assigned various meanings by fundamental and liberal theologians, scientists, and many, many others. It has become a "catch-all" phrase or a "power word" that means so many things to so many different people that at best it is a puzzling term and at worst it is a term of misunderstandings and disagreements. In order to prevent the misunderstandings and disagreements often generated by this term, it seems advantageous, especially with reference to the topic of this particular section (God), to try to define humanism as it is used in this study. In counseling, the term humanism means something drastically different from the phrase secular humanism that one encounters so often in this modern age. The term secular humanism seems to mean the total dependence of humankind on purely human resources to the exclusion of any need for a God of any type. This meaning is very different from counseling's use of the term humanism, especially as it is used in counseling's philosophical underpinnings. As used in counseling and in this study, humanism is meant to be understood as a simple label denoting those counseling theories which adopt a belief in humanity as a special entity and with a special identity. Humanism implies more than biological adaptations. It implies a unique and individual self in relation to other unique and individual selves. In humanism a person is not only produced or created, but that person is also a producer and a creator. These beliefs, when examined at their fundamental level, do not preclude the existence of a God, as the phrase secular humanism often seems to imply. In fact, when examined closely and logically, humanism's beliefs in being, knowing, and valuing strongly imply a necessary place for a supernatural God.

Perhaps the one idea uniting the many divergent streams of humanistic thought is the belief in a unique self. This is the focal point for both philosophy and counseling. The idea of self-realization (becoming or moving to self-perfection) is very important in humanism because it is without meaning except as a derivative term of comparison. In other words, self-realization derived from whose standards or perfection as compared to what standard? If one carries the examination of the essential nature of the self as revealed in most humanistic theories back to a starting point, one can only logically come to what is called in philosophy and theology the ontological argument for God's existence. This argument was first proposed by St. Anselm (1033–1109) and later refined by Descartes and Leibnitz. This argument is germane to the subject of counseling because the ontological, epistemological, and axiological positions taken by humanism logically lead to this ancient attempted "proof" of God's existence. It must be noted, though, that the term "proof" is a bit misleading because many philosophers and theologians (especially Kant) have pointed out the critical shortcomings in this argument. This study makes no attempt to justify, vindicate, or condemn the worth of this argument as a philosophical proposition. But to fully understand humanism's position with reference to God, this argument must be briefly examined because humanism's basic philosophical foundations logically extend to this starting point.

The ontological argument for God's existence totally depends on a definition of God as "something than which nothing greater can be conceived" (St. Anselm, ed. by Hicks, 1964, p. 23). This "something" exists so truly that one cannot think of it as nonexistent. Existence in reality is greater than mere mental imagery; therefore if God is defined as that which nothing greater can be conceived, then He must necessarily exist in reality because reality is greater than imagination. If the idea of something that is the greatest thing one can think of exists in the understanding (this is obvious because one can understand such a statement and, and if it is understood, then it exists in the understanding), then it cannot be the greatest thing one can think of if it exists *only* in the understanding. If it is the greatest thing, then it must exist in reality as well as in the understanding or it forfeits the title of "greatest." The fact that one has an idea of a perfect being necessitates that that perfect being exists (Butler, 1966). Humanist epistemology is somewhat similar to this idea. In this epistemology one is implicitly confronted by the fact of this something than which nothing greater can be conceived. If there is such a thing as a self and if this self can know or interpret any part of the surrounding world (and this seems very likely), then the world must be in tune to the idea of human selfhood. Since, to a degree, humans as selves can interpret reality, then the whole of reality must be a self also. Since nothing can be conceived to exist without being in relation to other things, then reality is seen to be a community of selves in relation to each other, and because we can conceive of a self greater than any other in our understanding, this self must exist in reality also and must be a part of this relationship and be that which makes reality capable of interpretation. This ultimate Self must also be the standard to which self-realization must be compared. The self moves (becoming) toward that ultimate Self (perfection). "Stated generally, this is to say that the world is intelligible. Intelligence in the human mind makes demands upon the world, and the world responds in the language of intelligence" (Butler, 1951, p. 266). How can human intelligence understand the world unless the world itself is also grounded in reason? This ultimate reason is provided by an ultimate Self.

Descartes (ed. Hicks, 1964) formed this same point on axiological grounds. He found that his own existence was a fact, a self-evident self, and his imperfection was a fact also because knowledge is superior to doubt and yet Descartes confessed his doubt and thus the fact of his own imperfection. If, in his imperfection, he could conceive of a perfect existence, then (as in Anselm's logic) there must exist in reality this perfect existence. Again, counseling's term self-realization speaks directly to this idea. One cannot know if one is becoming a "better" self unless one can conceive of a derivative ultimate Self (perfection) as a point of comparison. The key to humanist ideas as they are seen at the most fundamental level is the primacy of the self and the idea that ultimate reality must be a self also. There is nothing absolute but God, the ultimate Self. Like the part of a whole, humanity as individual selves cannot know reality, nor truth, nor goodness without recourse to the nature of this relationship to the absolute principles of an ultimate Self, a God. Humanity is neither already good nor evil in nature. Each person is a potential self and becomes either good or evil as the personal potentiality reveals itself in actuality. The ultimate Self is the standard. The further one removes oneself in actualities from the absolute standard, the self is conversely further removed from relation with the ultimate Self (Butler, 1951).

No one has explored the influence these ideas have for counseling more than Viktor Frankl. His view of counseling is centered on the specialized nature of the self. (Although Frankl prefers to use spirit or soul rather than self in his terminology, this is clearly a matter of semantics. The meanings of these terms as used by Frankl and this study are interchangeable.) Frankl (1959) contended that a spiritual orientation (a consciousness of one's self, other selves, and an ultimate Self) is required in order to maintain mental health and for direction in one's life. He calls for a psychotherapy that deals not only with the outer physical world of humanity, but also with the human spirit and the conscious self. In dealing with these concepts of spirituality, Frankl tries to show "the reality of an unconscious religious attitude and a relatedness to God" (Kung, 1978, p. 320). Many of humanity's emotional problems are caused by ignoring this spiritual nature and relatedness to God. Frankl's idea of counseling is to use traditional psychotherapeutical methods combined with an attempt to put people in touch with their own spiritual nature and to treat spiritual problems as well as physical and mental problems. More clearly than any other psychotherapist, Frankl has continually demanded "that psychotherapy face the spiritual questions, particularly the question of meaning and eventually also the question of God, in order not to evade the confrontation with theology" (Kung, 1978, p. 321). At the most fundamental level, these questions of meaning, truth, goodness, and God are those problems with which humanistic counseling grapples.

As was noted earlier in discussing humanism's ontological base, a view of the self that makes humanity's relationship to reality a special case over and above evolutionary, environmental, and conditioning constraints opens the way for an interpretation of ultimate meanings in all reality. Ultimate meanings are nothing more than the absolute principles (truth and goodness, for example) that philosophers have discussed for ages. Humanistic ideas make a place for such absolutes (as opposed to environmentalism's dependence on relativism) to explain the world. Lesser qualities cannot exist without reference to these absolute principles, just as a self is related to an ultimate Self. They are end points of comparison. Human beings compare things, goodness, for example, on the basis of an absolute standard. Humans comparatively state that this "thing" is better than that "thing" but this other "thing" is better still. Such comparisons cannot exist without ultimately encountering a final "best", a quality where nothing better exists. At least philosophically, humanism recognizes an absolute from which lesser qualities flow and to which they are compared. By its strong adherence to a concept of self and the implication of an ultimate Self, humanism implies that this Self is the source of all absolutes. Everything else is seen in relation to this standard.

A. E. Taylor (1903) studied the idea of an absolute standard and psychology's denouncement of such a standard as a result of its logical positivist heritage. He concluded that basically such denouncements used language "gimmicks" to play "fast and loose" with the truth. Earlier it was seen that Ayer was convinced that even religious people recognized that when something cannot be described one is bound to talk nonsense when attempting to describe it (Ayer, 1946). Taylor (1926) posed two answers to the above criticisms of Ayer. First, he claimed that it was not nonsense that one encountered so much difficulty in speaking of God. The difficulty did not point to nonsense. Rather, it pointed to the idea of the inadequacy of language. Our language has been primarily adapted to express our attitude toward the things of this world. A key contention of humanism is the transcendency or supernatural quality of God. Taylor (1926) contended that it was only logical for a language of this world to encounter extreme difficulties when trying to express qualities not of this world. This difficulty is encountered even between cultures past and present on earth. It is extraordinarily difficult to translate a word or a phrase into another language when the concept expressed by those specific words is unknown to the other culture. When that happens, we are reduced to using the best analogy possible. We say that "it is sort of like..." and then use a comparison known to that present culture. By using analogies one can never be sure that one is conveying the exact meanings cross-culturally. All one can do is contrive the best analogy possible and hope it conveys enough meaning for the hearers to understand the original concept that is not exactly translatable into their own culture's language. Taylor (1926) stated that linguistic translations between qualities of this world and transcendent qualities are even more difficult. But the difficulty is not the same as confessing that the transcendental qualities make no sense at all. These qualities can, to a point, be understood, but linguistic inadequacy hinders a total explanation of such qualities.

Secondly, Taylor (1926) pointed out that those who criticize the idea of a supernatural God "have not understood that the name of God is necessarily the 'ineffable' name" (Taylor, ed. John Hicks, 1964, p. 158). As far back as the beginnings of religion can be traced, the idea of God, even if it was seen as no more than an oddly shaped stone, did not mean just the strange or powerful. It also meant the "uncanny," that which does not belong to this everyday world. In The Problem of Pain, C. S. Lewis (1973) expanded on this idea of the uncanny. He illustrated the point by saying that

> suppose you were told there was a tiger in the next room: You would know...danger and would feel fear. But if you were told "there is a ghost in the next room," and believed it you would again...feel fear, but of a different kind. It would not be based on danger, for no one is primarily afraid of what a ghost may do to him... It is "uncanny" rather than dangerous, and the special kind of fear it excites may be called Dread... Now suppose you were told, "there is a mighty spirit in the room," and believed it. Your feelings would be even less like the fear of danger: but the disturbance would be profound. [This spirit would cause] an emotion which might be expressed in Shakespeare's words, "Under it my genius is rebuked." This feeling may be described as awe, and the object which excites it as the Numinous. (p. 5)
>
> When man passes from physical fear to dread and awe, he makes a sheer jump and apprehends something which could never be "given," as danger is, by the physical facts and logical deductions from them. Most attempts to explain the Numinous presuppose the thing to be explained—as when anthropologists derive it from fear of the dead, without explaining why dead men (assuredly the least dangerous kind of men) should have attracted this peculiar feeling... There seem, in fact, to be only two views we can hold about awe [the uncanny]. Either it is a mere twist in the human mind, corresponding to nothing

> objective and serving no biological function, yet showing no tendency to disappear from that mind at its fullest development in poet, philosopher, or saint: or else it is a direct experience of the really supernatural, to which the name Revelation might properly be given. (pp. 8–9)

Few members of humanity have not experienced emotions of this world that in their sheer strength made it difficult to express the emotions in language. This in no way, though, negates the reality or cause of those emotions. The difficulty of expressing ideas concerning a transcendent God also in no way negates the reality of such a Being.

> We may reasonably draw the conclusion that religion is just as much a unique characteristic and interest of humanity as love of truth, love of beauty, and love of country. The religious experience is no more to be dismissed as an illusion than the thinker's, the artist's, or the patriot's. (Taylor, ed. Hicks, 1964, p. 160)

Taylor also concluded that pointing to so-called religious aberrations (evils perpetrated in the name of religion) as reasons for its nonexistence is as foolish as saying that science is worthless because it wasted labor on trying to square the circle, or saying that love is useless because of the pain incurred when it is foolishly bestowed.

> We are neither to suppose that there is no way to God because some ways which have been found promising at first led astray, nor yet that because there is a way, any way that mankind have tried must be as good a road to the goal as any other. (Taylor, ed. Hicks, 1964, p. 161)

If God's name is the ineffable name, as Taylor and other humanists contend, that accounts for the difficulty incurred in such a discussion. Logically, one could expect nothing else.

This point of logic and ineffability is very important. Ayer (1946) concluded that, logically, when one speaks of the ineffable the resulting description must be nonsensical. C. S. Lewis (1973) pointed out the singular error in this "logic."

> His Omnipotence means power to do all that is intrinsically possible, not to do the intrinsically impossible. You may attribute miracles to Him, but not nonsense. [Equally, human beings are not being nonsensical in their inability to express the

> ineffable.] If you choose to say, "God can give a creature free will and at the same time withhold free will from it," you have not succeeded in saying *anything* about God: meaningless combinations of words do not suddenly acquire meaning simply because we prefix to them the two other words "God can." It remains true that all *things* are possible with God: the intrinsic impossibilities are not things but nonentities. It is no more possible for God than for the weakest of His creatures to carry out both of two mutually exclusive alternatives; not because His power meets an obstacle, but because nonsense remains nonsense even when we talk about God. (p. 16)

Seeing God as the ineffable is not such a logical contradiction. This idea admits expressional difficulties but says nothing else about the reality of such a Being. Humanists realize this difficulty but believe it is, to a degree, minimized by God's revelatory nature. We understand, not because He is any less ineffable, but because He reveals things to us. We understand such revelations because our selves are minutely tuned to the same key as His Self, or phrased Biblically, because we are made in His image. (This is one reason that the self is treated with such respect in humanistic counseling theories.) The essence of the human self is what it is because of its relation to an Ultimate Self. This relation, a priori and intuited, is the basis of our understanding of questions of ultimacy. The ineffability causes expressional problems, not problems of understanding or belief.

Humanism believes that there is no justification for dismissing the idea of a supernatural God simply because such an idea generates expressional difficulties and also because such an idea is not revealed through the physical senses. The concept of the reversibility or irreversibility of time is also not revealed through the senses. No experiment has been designed to observe or verify such a proposition, but the proposition still exists in the mind and, indeed, plays a part in Einsteinian physics. This concept is not dismissed because of the difficulties involved in linguistically expressing it, nor is it dismissed because it is not derived through the senses. The concept of God is also not to be dismissed on this basis. At its philosophic base, humanism admits that there are many problems revealed when humanity encounters the idea of God. But humanity should not dismiss the idea because of such difficulties. "The consciousness of knowing little need not beget a distrust of that which he does know" (Paley, ed. Hicks, 1964, p. 103).

The foundational points of humanism, its ontology, epistemology, and axiology implicitly form a logical path to a supernatural Being. Ontologically, the idea of a self that is capable of interpreting reality will not hold up unless some provision is made for that reality to be structured like the self. In order to be capable of interpretation (and humanism believes in just this point), then ultimate reality must be a Self also. Giving this Self ultimate qualities removes Him from the natural order as a transcendent Being. We have an understanding, however slight, of this Being because our essential selves are tuned to the same key as the ultimate Self.

Epistemologically, the path to an idea of God follows the belief that this world and this universe have qualities and meanings that humans can comprehend. How can a self get meaning and quality out of the world unless some Self invests it with those very meanings and qualities? There must be an ultimate Mind who puts these meanings into the world. The existence of objective meanings in the world implies some kind of "mental life" as the core of reality. Meaning cannot be detached from this mind without becoming unintelligible (Butler, 1966). "Selfhood being what it is, and the surrounding world being so well tuned to the experience of self, it is believed then that reality is a Self" (Butler, 1966, p. 67).

Axiologically, one finds, as Kant did, a belief in an essential self which contains as part of its nature an obligation to moral law that is directed toward the end of achieving moral perfection. Kant believed that this made it necessary that there be a Supreme Being who instilled us with this moral obligation. He reasoned that the moral law requires obedience, but in this natural world there is no guarantee that contentment shall accompany obedience. It is a necessity, therefore, that a higher order than the natural world must exist, a society of moral selves and a Supreme Being to serve as a reason (a guarantor of contentment) for obeying this moral law.

Humanists accept the idea that a scientific proof for God's existence does not at this time exist because He is not perceived through the senses nor can He be observed, measured, or verified sensationally. But humanists reject the idea that these scientific methods are the only acceptable parameters one can use in discussing God's nature. Humanism, at least philosophically, makes a place for the existence of subjective knowledge, for a unique personal self, and for absolute principles. It was earlier inferred that these three ideas logically lead to the idea of a Supreme Being. In truth, though, that is examining the issue backwards. If one starts with a conception of a supernatural, ultimate Being, then one is led to a belief in a special nature for humans, a belief that they can interpret ultimate qualities, and a belief that they can understand, and, to a degree, follow absolute principles.

A Brief Summary of the Philosophic Differences between Environmentalism and Humanism

The movements of environmentalism and humanism are so opposed to one another at the level of their philosophical assumptions that one can readily note the basic differences, and this section is meant only as a summary or encapsulation of the preceding discussion.

Environmentalism's ontological principles are deeply rooted in that comparatively modern philosophy known as logical positivism. The advent of a prestigious place for the natural sciences in recent times is a concomitant development of this positivistic influence. In this belief, humanity's "being" depends on biological, evolutionary, and environmental factors only. This being is investigated with the same objective stance as would be given any natural phenomenon. All forms of subjectivity are disallowed because subjectivism is not verifiable nor is it allowable under the terms of the modern scientific method. The sensory world is the only reality available, and this reality can only be perceived and understood through the physical senses. An idea of any absolute reality is dismissed and replaced with an idea of a thoroughly relative reality that changes due to environmental and evolutionary constraints. In this reality, human beings have little, if any, freedom of choice.

In humanism, an objective reality based on the physical senses is allowed, but humanism differs in that it claims that this is not the whole of reality. Rather, the humanists believe that a subjective reality also exists. This subjective reality is preeminent over any objective reality because all objective reality is perceived and filtered through a conscious subjective self that gives meaning to the objective reality. This idea of self is the keystone of humanism. This self is seen as special and unique over and above environmental and evolutionary factors. It possesses an a priori structure of consciousness that invests meaning to reality because it is tuned to the same key as reality. Through this innate structure and reflection and intuition and other subjective means, the self can interpret the ultimate quality of reality. These ideational abstractions are not subject to the scientific method nor to revelation through the physical senses. Because reality is at least partially interpretable by a self, the humanists feel that this is evidence for the idea that reality itself must then also be a self. Whereas environmentalism sees a relative character for reality, the humanists recognize qualities of absolute character. It is humankind's a priori essence, the self, that alone is able to interpret such absolutes. This relation to absolute reality is the quality that makes humanity special and unique. In this relation, free choice is not forbidden.

Because of the pragmatic influence, environmental epistemology follows the idea that all knowledge is restricted to external, experiential phenomena. The scientific method and the physical senses thus become the only path to knowledge. This further means that all knowledge must then become the sole province of the natural sciences. Knowledge is seen as a problem to be solved. Any relative solution that "works" (solves the problem) is said to constitute knowledge and truth. Experience is therefore the final test of knowledge, and truth can only be achieved empirically. It is not absolute but relative to each given experience. The emphasis is always on the object of knowledge. Since the whole of reality cannot be known, the process of knowing involves gradually paring away at a specific part of reality until that single relative part is clear. In terms of how one learns, environmentalism recognizes only one method; all learning is seen in terms of conditioning principles.

As in their theories of being, all humanistic theories epistemologically insist on the validity of subjective knowledge. The first and only sure knowledge that one has is the knowledge of one's own existence. All other knowledge is filtered through this subjective knowledge. Sensation itself (knowledge through the senses) is a process of passive receptivity and chaos and is invested with meaning only through a person's innate conscious structure, a self. Such a self can create new facts and ideas not limited to those revealed through the senses. Knowledge is thus more than empiricism. It is intuition, reflection, and a priori essences that form the conscious being. Through this subjectivity, ultimate qualities can be known and the idea of absolutes (such as truth) can be apprehended. The conscious self examines the whole of reality and innately perceives that knowledge of the parts is only meaningful in reference to this whole. Humanists also believe in the idea that knowledge is based on experience, but on the experience of perception by a conscious self, not on the experience of sensation, as proposed by the environmentalists.

The basic ideas of environmental axiology reflect a belief in the idea of relative moral democracy, the greatest good for the greatest number. Values are seen in terms of hedonism (that which keeps or returns an organism to a state of comfort) and utility. Values are exactly like any other form of learned behavior and the "right" values can be taught through conditioning principles (extinguishing maladaptive values and rewarding appropriate values). The principles of science are very useful in deriving and continuing proper value systems. Values are not inner-directed nor necessarily even purposeful. There is no "built-in" sense of goodness or morality. Also, there is no such thing as absolute value. Value is subject to the relativity of each given experience. Seen in this way, "right" is what a particular society agrees to call right and is purely relative to the end that particular society has in mind. In this way, "good" and "evil" can only be seen in a social setting and are totally dependent on the reinforcers meted out by a society.

In humanism, value and goodness can only be seen in reference to an idea of absolute goodness. It is a referential examination that is comparatively traced back to a goodness that is called the "best." Such comparative values are founded on intuition and essential moral insights incorporated in the human conscious self. The goal of a morality based on absolute qualities is the perfection of self and the subsequent perfection of society. Universal moral laws are an innate part of human nature and also part of that self that makes humankind unique and special. As one is attuned to these moral laws and moves toward them, meaning is revealed in this quest for self (and societal) realization. Neither science nor the senses are equipped to answer questions of right and wrong. A conscious self attempting to approach the absolute ground of goodness is much better equipped, according to humanism, to make such value decisions.

On the level of philosophical assumptions, environmentalism rejects the idea of God as He is most often conceived in mainstream theology. A naturalistic idea of god is more permissible. If a god is to exist, he must be subject to the same laws, phenomena, and causal factors that determine the rest of existence. The "normal" idea of a supernatural God cannot be interpreted through the senses or scientifically verified and must therefore be rejected. In many ways, modern science answers most of the questions that in past times were not understood and therefore attributable to some form of supernaturalism. Because of science, no subjective "higher court" need be appealed to any longer by modern humanity. There simply are no transcendent or absolute realities.

On the level of its philosophical assumptions, humanism makes a logical, though subjective, case for a supernatural God as being identical with ultimate Reality. Humanism also makes its case that this ultimate Reality is a Self and that a human self is in some way related to this Self. All absolute standards flow from this ultimate Reality. Expressional difficulties are inherent in a discussion of such a Reality because of the inadequacy of a nontranscendent language in expressing a transcendent Being, and also because this transcendent Being is, by definition, ineffable except as He chooses to reveal His nature to humanity. Such a Being is not subject to the "proof" of the physical sciences nor principles of sensory verifiability. The fact that human selves are somehow in tune to His Self provides the basis for a relation of human beings to Reality. Ultimate meaning for humanism is provided through their ideas concerning God's nature.

Similarities in Environmentalism and Humanism

In the examination of the present counseling debate between humanism and environmentalism, it is apparent that the controversy exists because of the irreconcilable differences between these two movements. In fact, the deeper one investigates (back to the level of philosophical assumptions), the more one notices the irreconcilable nature of these differences. Despite these acute differences, however, it still remains a fact that on some points and some levels there are a few similarities. In the most general fashion, the most obvious similarity is, of course, the basic motivating goal, the "raison d'etre", of each movement. Both humanism and environmentalism seek to help the human condition as individuals and as a society. This truism may be so simplistic to some that it borders on being a worthless statement. But this is not necessarily the case. Humanism and environmentalism differ on how help should be offered. They differ on theory, on method, on process, and on terms of evaluation of the process, but it may be that the single goal of "wanting to help" makes the two movements more similar than all the specific disparities make them different. The desire to help, to improve the lot of humanity, should not be devalued because of its simplicity. Though they may take radically different paths to achieve their purpose, it would be a terrible error to forget the purpose itself is, for both movements, the same. This single idea makes humanism and environmentalism part of the same force, the same helping profession, and insures that regardless of the differences, they are "professional brothers" and not professional antagonists.

Though it is often difficult to isolate other specific similarities, many of those involved in counseling and philosophy believe that such similarities can exist and on some level can make the two movements more compatible. Norman Malcolm (ed. Wann, 1964) found many distressing problems with environmentalism but also recognized a hard core of logical truth at its base. Carl Rogers (ed. Wann, 1964) stated that there was much about environmentalism that he could accept. R. B. MacLeod (ed. Wann, 1964) said that in his opinion approaching the two movements as antagonists or alternatives was incorrect. He felt that they were simply two interesting approaches to the same problem. Skinner (ed. Wann, 1964) confessed that he believed that internal states do exist and that part of human progress could be credited to the improved description of such things. He further stated that no process or entity is to be rejected purely on the grounds that it is subjective or mental. Even Rudolph Carnap (eds. Feigl & Scriven, 1956), the logical positivist and founder of the doctrine of physicalism which exerted great influence on environmental thought, admitted that awareness of one's own state of feelings and imaginings should be recognized as a kind of observation and therefore a legitimate source of knowledge. Rogers (ed. Wann, 1964) summarized these conciliatory statements when he noted that a mature psychological science must use both subjective and objective (humanistic and environmentalistic) means appropriately interwoven so that a satisfactory behavioral science can emerge.

Though few in number, there exists an ample amount of similarities to reach some level of mutual understanding. Barclay (1971) saw the humanistic-environmental division in terms very much like the middle-age conflict of faith versus reason (which was itself yet another extension of the metaphysical-antimetaphysical debate). Though there were opposing points of view on some issues of faith and reason, many people (in fact, all but the extremists) believed that the terms were not logically contradictory but were compatible on some points. Barclay (1968) argued for humanism and environmentalism also to be examined in this light. He felt that many characteristics were differences when examined in terms of degree but were similarities when examined in terms of kind. For example, environmentalism seems to be more precise in specifying independent variables because of its emphasis on observability. This is a difference in degree. It is more precise than humanism, but it is not a difference in kind because in point of fact both environmentalism and humanist are often (because of the very nature of independent variables) imprecise in gauging the role of independent variables. This imprecision is indeed a similarity and makes it impossible, at least in this area, for either movement to claim infallibility and thus superiority. Rogers (ed. Wann, 1964) echoed this idea that imprecision draws the two movements closer together in terms of similarity when he noted that

> there is no special virtue attached to the policy of limiting our theories to observable behavior. Neither, I would add, is there any *inherent* virtue in basing our theorizing on phenomenological variables. (p. 129)

In either case the task of evaluation is formidable.

Barclay (1971) identified what he believed to be certain problem areas that promulgated the humanism-environmentalism conflict and acted as a hindrance to identifying areas of similarities and compatibilities between them. One such reason is the fact that many, if not most, psychology departments view with outright contempt the scholastic effort to delve into the history and philosophy of psychology. Scriven (ed. Wann, 1964) referred to this process as the "shotgun divorce" of psychology and philosophy. In addition to making similarities and areas of compatibility more likely to remain obscure, this process makes each new generation of beginning psychologists (and counselors) more prone to repeat the same historical and philosophical errors and more prone to carry on the divisiveness within the field. Barclay (1968) felt that psychology and counseling departmental allegiances toward one side or the other, humanism or environmentalism, takes on almost religious overtones and insures that "one side" will know little of "the other" and will cavalierly ignore those complex similarities that could lead toward compatibility. Scriven (ed. Wann, 1964) made this same point and additionally said that psychology fails to recognize that both movements have two limitations. One limitation is the idea that a colossal quantity of psychological information has been incorporated as a stock part of truisms that most of the general populace knows about human behavior. In other words, the territory of psychology is, to a degree, restricted by common sense. Another limitation is that, for better or worse, many of psychology's novel ideas have been, and are now being, constantly annexed by other sciences, such as biochemistry, neurophysiology, and others. If psychology also deprives itself of its history and the discussion of philosophical issues, then it will continue its conflicts and, professionally, it will be bereft of all goals and its promising future.

In place of this potential bleakness, Barclay (1971) called for the profession to ignore the recurring American educational tendency to select a simple, single system that supposedly would work in every case and instead allow both systems, humanism and environmentalism, to develop to their full potential (and that includes their philosophy) and not choose one over the other. Then perhaps a taxonomy could be developed on research grounds to try to determine which procedure seems to work best on which problem and with which individual. This seems possible because the environmental approach has a singularly powerful potential for administering to specific kinds of client needs with specific behavior change processes. Humanism, on the other hand, has a deep concern for understanding the client and communicating to this client a way to engage in self-exploration and self-concept and personal feeling examinations. "Each strategy possesses a definite power potential for coping with specific kinds of problems in counseling" (Barclay, 1968, p. 49). When counseling, as a field of study, examines its history and its philosophy, there will not be a synthesis of all theories into one unified field theory; the drastic difference at the level of philosophical assumptions precludes such a total synthesis. But it will make it easier for psychologists and counselors to identify similarities and potential points of compatibility between the theories. This can only benefit those who make use of counseling services.

As earlier noted, most of these similarities and compatibilities will be apparent at the level of practice and methodology. For example, Frankl, a humanist, identified one of his techniques with the appellation "de-reflection." This is an attempt to counteract a compulsive inclination toward self-observation, or compulsive observation of an obsessive fear. The basic idea is to gradually reduce the importance of the self-observation so that the compulsion and obsessive quality is also gradually reduced (Frankl, 1973). Though developed by a thoroughly humanistic practitioner, this technique, at least on the level of methodology, is remarkably similar to Joseph Wolpe's purely environmental technique of "systematic desensitization". With this technique one's compulsive fears are gradually reduced by gradually (in successive stages) confronting this compulsive fear until it ceases to inspire fear. Environmentalists claim that other humanistic methods, such as Rogers' highly verbal client-centered techniques, are only thinly veiled attempts at verbal conditioning and are actually examples of actively restructuring a client's environment through subtle offers of environmental contingencies (reinforcements). Humanists say that the success of many environmental techniques is the result of the subjective relationship (based on verbal cues, etc.) between the counselor and client. In other words, both movements often attribute success to one another because each believes the other to be practicing the same technique, though each erroneously insists on disbelieving this and also persists in labeling such techniques as purely humanistic or purely environmentalistic.

Both movements are also similar in their quest for evaluatory methods. Many environmentalists see humanists as mystics making esoteric pronouncements and generating no sound (empirically verifiable) results whatsoever. This is not the case. The only evaluatory discrepancy between the two is the fact that humanists believe that subjective methods can be evaluated and environmentalists deny this. But both methods are similar because they know that to go forward there must be processes of evaluation. Carl Rogers (ed. Wann, 1964) called for a concentrated effort by all humanists to, as objectively as possible, evaluate every scrap of data. Barclay (1971) suggested that humanism would develop only as it continued to develop rigorous and, when possible, objective evaluation criteria, and he also challenged environmentalists to be more willing to turn their objective standards to subjective phenomena. This similarity of evaluation is not new. Edmund Husserl

(Spiegelberg, 1960), the so-called father of phenomenology, saw it as the science where perception and subjective phenomena could often be examined in the same rigorously objective, scientific light as natural phenomena.

Humanism and environmentalism can find some accommodations: in method, in limitations, in subject matter, in goals, in practice, and in evaluation. It would be to counseling's advantage to pursue such accommodations. Although it is true that the bulk of this study is devoted to an examination of the philosophical foundations of these two movements (at this level, the differences are keen and the accommodations are few), on the level of common sense and actual treatment, there are compatibilities that are worthy of investigation and possible partial synthesis. As a whole, the field of counseling could only prosper by such investigations.

Chapter IV

B. F. Skinner

In the previous chapters several philosophical and counseling threads have been introduced. Basically, these topics have taken the following forms: a brief review of the philosophical argument of metaphysics versus antimetaphysics; an attempt to relate this philosophic argument to the environmental versus humanism conflict in modern counseling; and the identification of the major philosophical constructs undergirding the respective counseling movements. The purpose of this chapter is to attempt to tie these threads into some sort of intelligible conclusion by examining the specific counseling concepts of Viktor Frankl and B. F. Skinner and relating these concepts to their philosophic roots. The philosophical threads so far examined play a great role in influencing and shaping the field of counseling. By examining the works of a theorist representing each side of the counseling conflict, the attempt will be made to show the influence that the previously identified philosophic framework exerts on specific counseling theories, theorists, and, to a lesser degree, practices.

The specific counseling ideas of Frankl and Skinner are directly traceable to the basic concepts of being, knowing, and valuing that form the foundation of the respective theories. These counseling precepts and the practices born of these precepts reflect a particular philosophical birthright. For example, when Frankl makes a statement concerning the relationship of human responsibility to the idea of free choice, he is, in part, revealing his theory about human nature and in turn this theory reveals his philosophy regarding ontology. Frankl's and Skinner's words will reveal their philosophy and this will in turn reveal the consistency of the boundaries of the theories and practices that they espouse. One cannot truly know the "why" of these theoretical and practical concepts unless one also knows the framework from which these concepts emanate. Relating Frankl's and Skinner's words to the previously identified ontological, epistemological, and axiological constructs provides a closure of sorts. It reveals the necessary relationship between philosophy, theory, and practice. Counseling must give equal weight to each section of this triad if it is to successfully defend itself against its many detractors. Skinner's theory of behavior and behavior change very consistently reflects the antimetaphysical-environmental heritage of philosophy. It is doubtful, though, that Skinner would acknowledge this fact. To him, this idea would not be so much erroneous as it would be irrelevant. He felt that psychology and counseling expend far too little energy solving specific problems, which is, after all (to Skinner at least), the single purpose of the field. His theories have produced specific operationalistic tendencies to address specific problems. Because of his influence most works on environmental counseling have

> become compendiums of technique and methods. They are not systematic in the sense that [anyone] has adopted a theoretical point of view, developed its philosophy and assumptions, and presented techniques derived from, or consistent with, the assumptions and theory. (Patterson, 1980, p. 105)

This chapter makes just such an attempt: to systematically examine the theories and practices inherent in Skinner's writing and to examine the assumptions from which they are derived.

For Skinner, reality has a very narrow area of interpretation. It is simply that body of empirical knowledge which has resulted from the application of the experimental method to the sensational world. His profession, psychology, is an exact microcosm of this larger reality. It is the application of the experimental method in psychology in order to explain the genesis and maintenance of abnormal patterns of behavior and to use this information to treat and prevent such "abnormalities" by means of controlled experimental conditioning techniques (Yates, 1970). The object of these experiments is of course humanity itself. In the book *About Behaviorism*, Skinner (1976) echoed the ontological premise that lies at the heart of all antimetaphysical and environmental pronouncements: "the human species...begins and remains a biological system, and the behavioristic position is that it is nothing more than that" (p. 49). Although superficially a simple enough statement, this Skinnerian quote actually identifies humanity's place in the two major components of reality known as time and space. Humanity occupies a niche in space in a biological order that is limited to strictly observable and definable phenomena. Furthermore, the species exists in a nontranscendent time reference capable of total quantification and subject only to natural laws. There is no "soul" and no "mind" (in the specialized philosophic sense). There is only a biologic organism that is a chance product of evolution and environmental contingencies that exists only in the "here and now." Consequently, this biological entity is devoid of motive and purpose (in any self-directed way). Skinner (1976) claimed that no one was self-directed. He believed that when one claimed to be aware of self, or aware of one's purpose, it was only a linguistic misnomer. A person cannot "have" a purpose. One can only be "given" a purpose when the environment is reinforcing in a certain manner. Purpose is a condition produced by reinforcement, and without an environment dispensing these reinforcers, there can be no such thing as purpose.

The term responsibility is viewed in this same light. To Skinner, humans are not responsible. The basis of this proposition is found in the deterministic pronouncements of environmentalism's philosophical assumptions. If reality is a world of physical phenomena and each part of that reality, including humankind, is what it is (finds its defining criteria in natural evolutionary or environmental contingencies) only because of certain physical forces, then the idea of responsibility becomes logically impossible because the concept of choice is negated. Each part of reality does what it does because of the natural forces that have determined its nature. The first "casualty" of this line of thought has to be a sense of responsibility for experiential consequences. Skinner (1976) claimed that society is in error to state that a person is ever responsible for anything. Rather, reality

> holds him responsible by maintaining environmental contingencies and [it] holds him accountable in the more general sense of keeping an account of his behavior to see whether it meets the specifications upon which escape from punishment may be contingent. It does not follow that he *has* a responsibility; the simple fact is that certain kinds of contingencies have affected him. If they have failed to do so, it is because he is uncontrollable, not because he is irresponsible. (Skinner, 1976, pp. 205–206)

The term controllability is thus proper usage, responsibility is not.

In denying the existence of goals, inner directions, purposes, and responsibilities, Skinner is simply and logically following the ontological dictates of the environmental view of self. In terms of counseling theory and practice, perhaps the key ontological point is this disavowal of the self by one position and the adoption of the self by the other position. All environmental theories and practices must be constructed without recourse to a unique essential self because the philosophical assumptions make no place for such a self in the movement. This has far-reaching theoretical consequences because without a self there can be no acceptable emphasis on subjectivity, no innate (a priori) qualities, and no ultimate qualities. There can only be the physically phenomenal world and the contact one can maintain with that world through one's physical senses. "I know of no essentially human feature that has been shown to be beyond the reach of scientific analysis" (Skinner, 1976, p. 263). "There is no place in the scientific position for a self as a true originator or initiator of action" (Skinner, 1976, p. 248). Skinner (1976) argued that what people normally refer to as a self is simply an organism that is labeled a person or self as it acquires a repertoire of behavior. "But all selves are the products of genetic and environmental histories" (Skinner, 1976, p. 247). Skinner (1976) relegated all such concepts of self (self-image, self-knowledge, self-management, etc.) as part of a behavioral repertoire that must be attributed to reinforcing contingencies.

The concept of originality, the production of new ideas, is attributed to a behavioral repertoire also and is dependent, like all behavior, on reinforcing contingencies, not original thoughts. Though humanists see originality as an integral part of a self, Skinner stated that other and better explanations were available. Although the humanists tend to believe that

> Man is now in much better control of the world than were his ancestors, and this suggests a progress in discovery and invention in which there appears to be a strong element of originality. But we [the environmentalists] could express the fact just as well by saying that the environment is now in better control of man. Reinforcing contingencies shape the behavior of the individual, and novel contingencies generate novel forms of behavior. (Skinner, 1953, p. 255)

Thus, new ideas are not "created" by a self. They are arranged and they happen to an organism because of new patterns of reinforcement. Skinner (1953) felt that this dissolution of the concept of an innate self was one of the chief contributions of his science of human behavior. The removal of this idea of self makes the environmental experiments dealing with animals and with statistical manipulations directly relevant to humans. The quantifiable and observable results of psychological experimentation (such as those using Skinner boxes) are only extendible to humans if the humans are like the animals (a simple biologic and evolutionary entity) undergoing the tests. If a person has a unique self that acts as the point of differentiation between humans and the other animals, then that insures that much of the results of animal experimentation would be of little value. Without such a self, humans are subject to environmental contingencies exactly in the same way as the rest of physical reality and experimental results would be interchangeably referable to each part of such a reality.

Skinner also dealt with another key environmental foundational concept in his writings. He adopted a theory in which the physical senses and modern science would replace the idea of self in explaining human behavior. He stated that if psychology is a "science of the behavior of organisms, human or otherwise, then it is part of biology, a natural science for which tested and highly successful methods are available" (Skinner, ed. Wann, 1964, p. 79). These methods according to Skinner are far superior to attributing explanations to mystically innate subjective behaviors. "The techniques available to such a science give an empirical theory of knowledge [and reality] certain advantages over theories derived from philosophy and logic" (Skinner, ed. Wann, 1964, p. 84). These advantages largely result from the observability and objective verifiability inherent in empiricism. This reality need not be subject to introspective investigation. Instead, objective measurements can show reality, changes in reality, and human interaction through sensory processes within reality. Skinner labeled this a simpler and more accurate basis on which to develop a theory of behavior.

> So far as behavior is concerned, both sensation and perception may be analyzed as forms of stimulus control. The subject need not be regarded as observing or evaluating conscious experience. (Skinner, ed. Wann, 1964, p. 89)

He saw reality as a world of sensation and experience rather than a world of conscious thought, and his behavioral theories reflect this belief. "Rather than describe experiments with the terminology of introspection, we may formulate them in their proper place in experimental analysis [empiricism]" (Skinner, ed. Wann, 1964, p. 90).

In terms of epistemology, Skinner's writings reveal a behavioral theory deeply grounded in those environmental foundations identified in the previous chapter. In fact, the bulk of his theories and practices are seen more in terms of epistemological concerns rather than either concepts of being or valuing. The phrase one most often sees in Skinner's work is operant conditioning. This is the key idea in his psychological strategies, and it has exerted the greatest influence on other environmental thinkers following him. Operant conditioning is a learning principle based on therapeutic interventions designed to rearrange contingent behavioral consequences in order to alter undesired behaviors or to remedy behavioral deficiencies (Patterson, 1980).

Patterson (1980) identified four basic characteristics of the operant conditioning model as developed by Skinner and used by each succeeding generation of environmental counselors. These four characteristics strongly reflect the philosophical assumptions of environmental epistemology. The first characteristic is that the operant model is empirical, and internal states are considered to be irrelevant. Also, this model is a practical engineering approach and hypotheses are tested in experience through the variation of consequences. The operant model is relative in that the analysis of a single case is emphasized and results are for that single case only and are not referable to other cases until the analysis is replicated in every case. Finally, the operant model is concerned with the present. It is sufficient to deal with the present disturbing behavior and modify it with current reinforcers without regard to the original determinants of the problem (Patterson, 1980). These four theoretical and practical characteristics are in perfect alignment with the fundamental assumptions of environmental knowledge. The characteristics stress the problem-solving nature of the philosophy. The pragmatic approach (whatever works in an experience is the solution and the truth) is also stressed. Emphasis is also placed on the scientific verifiability of the model, and also emphasis is placed on paring away at the whole of reality and only working with one small part of it.

These theories and methods are products of Skinner's writings based on his adoption of the philosophical concepts underlying them. He (1976) espoused principles, theories, and practices to "deal exclusively with external events and turn attention away from self-observation and self-knowledge" (p. 18). Internal events cannot be empirically dealt with and are to be dismissed.

> Mental life and the world in which it is lived are inventions. They have been invented on the analogy of external behavior occurring under external contingencies. Thinking is behaving. The mistake is allocating the behavior to the mind. (Skinner, 1976, p. 115)

"The behavior which we call knowing is due to a particular kind of differential reinforcement" (Skinner, 1953, p. 287). Patterson (1980) supplied a brief summary of environmental epistemology in the field of counseling and once again one notices the exact parallels to its philosophical foundations. The behavioral learning models

> have developed out of laboratory studies, with emphasis on observation and manipulation of objective events and reduction of complex variables into simpler components. (p. 215)

In terms of learning, knowledge, and truth, Skinner is a major source of influence in counseling. The following principles reflect his basic ideas that dominate environmental epistemology: The focus of learning is behavior. This means only overt actions that can be described in objective terms without recourse to theoretical constructs or concepts. The task of counseling is to change deviant behavior symptoms and hypothetical personality structures are to be ignored. Thinking and knowing are both examples of learned behaviors and are subject to the same conditions that shape all other classes of behaviors, i.e., biological forces and environmental contingencies. The methods of inquiry common to all natural sciences are also the best methods to investigate a science of human behavior. The final environmental point states that the proper basis for a program of behavior modification deals only with current behaviors while antecedent behaviors are basically considered irrelevant (Patterson, 1980). These theoretical characteristics of environmentalism directly reflect the ideas of knowledge derived from the philosophical foundations inherited from antimetaphysical assumptions. Skinner's conception of a science of human behavior is directly in line with the tradition of the empiricists (Locke and Hume), the positivists (Ayer and Carnap), and the pragmatists (Dewey and Peirce). Skinner's writings, especially about the process of knowing, continually reflect this heritage.

In his version of a science of behavior, Skinner's views of epistemology have been quite explicit. For example, subjective knowledge is disallowed.

> A science of subjective experience would have no more bearing on a science of behavior than a science of what people feel about fire would have on the science of combustion... A physical world generates both physical action and the physical conditions within the body to which a person responds when a verbal community arranges the necessary contingencies. No special kind of mind stuff is assumed. (Skinner, 1976, p. 243)

This theme is repeated over and over in his works, just as it is continually repeated in the works of Locke, Ayer, Dewey, and Darwin. A person can know only what the senses (one's physical or biological nature) can reveal. The environment thus makes humans what they are and they possess no innate mental nature to act on this environment or to restructure it in any a priori fashion.

> The greatest achievements of the human species (not of the human mind) have occurred too recently to make a genetic explanation defensible, but whether we appeal to contingencies of survival or contingencies of reinforcement we can at least dispense with the appeal to innate ideas. It may be true that there is no structure without construction, but we must look to

> the constructing environment, not to a constructing mind. (Skinner, 1976, p. 129)

"Our perception of the world—our knowledge of it—is our behavior with respect to the world" (Skinner, 1953, p. 140).

By disallowing subjectivity, Skinner opens the way for the environmental concept of knowledge in counseling. Phrased as simply as possible, this concept is the process of solving a problem in an overt and pragmatic manner. Kanfer and Phillips (1970) explained the process in two stages: to first locate the problem and then attack that problem until it no longer exists. The therapeutic goals are defined by society and its agents and not by any theory underlying the modification process itself. "Problem solving may be defined as any behavior which, through the manipulation of variables, makes the appearance of a solution more probable" (Skinner, 1953, p. 247). A problem that has been solved represents our closest proximity to what is called knowledge. "The result of solving a problem is the appearance of a solution in the form of a response. The response alters the situation so that the problem disappears" (Skinner, 1953, p. 252). This process can never be absolute in nature. What works in one case may not work in the next. Since problem solving is the only knowledge attainable, then knowledge itself cannot have an absolute quality. It is relative to each experience, each stimulus, and each response. "The relation between the preliminary behavior and the appearance of the solution is simply the relation between the manipulation of variables and the emission of a response" (Skinner, 1953, p. 252). This is as much of knowledge as a human being can achieve and there is nothing absolute in this process. Skinner's writings usually take special care to emphasize the idea that knowledge and truth are relative commodities and can only be understood in the frame of reference of a particular society in a particular point in time.

> The truth of a statement of fact is limited by the sources of the behavior of the speaker, the control exerted by the current setting, the effects of similar settings in the past, the effects upon the listener leading to precision or to exaggeration or falsification, and so on. There is no way in which a verbal description of a setting can be absolutely true... The verbal community of the scientist maintains special sanctions in an effort to guarantee validity and objectivity but, again, there can be no absolute. No deduction from a rule or law can therefore be absolutely true. Absolute truth can be found, if at all, only in rules derived from rules, and here it is mere tautology. (Skinner, 1976, p. 150)

A theory of counseling resulting from these principles would be a "shotgun" approach. Patterson (1980) stated that environmentalists

> make a virtue out of necessity in expressing their willingness to try anything that seems to work or that might work. Thus specific techniques are being tried, recommended, and accepted on a superstitious basis until they are extinguished after enough failures. (p. 248)

An epistemology based on relativity virtually insures a technique oriented science of behavior, but it does not insure an integrating theory to tie the many methods and techniques together. "While there are many techniques, there are few concepts or general principles involved in behavior therapy" (Ullman & Krasner, 1969, p. 252). Such therapy seems to be based on "a nontheoretical amalgam of pragmatic principles" (Weitzman, 1967, p. 303). These "pragmatic principles" are strictly derived from a foundation of knowing that classifies knowledge as that which works (relieves symptoms) in a specific time and a specific experience.

Environmental theories and practices are built on these foundational beliefs and remain consistent with the assumptions that form the environmental heritage. Also, as has been seen in the arguments of the antimetaphysicians, the logical product of such a theory of knowledge is a belief in science as the only real possessor of anything that could be referred to as knowledge. Skinner's thoughts represent a continuation of this heritage:

> What we need is a technology of behavior. We could solve our problems quickly enough if we could adjust the growth of the world's population as precisely as we adjust the course of a spaceship. (Skinner, 1971, p. 5)

Skinner seems to suggest that as the methods of the behavioral sciences become more and more like the methods of the physical sciences, then and only then will a worthwhile science of behavior develop. As noted in an earlier chapter, this belief is tantamount to acknowledging that scientific knowledge is the only knowledge worth having because it is the only form of knowledge possible.

> We can follow the path taken by physics and biology by turning directly to the relation between behavior and the environment and neglecting supposed mediating states of mind. Physics did

> not advance by looking more closely at the jubilance of a falling body, or biology by looking at the nature of vital spirits, and we do not need to try to discover what personalities, states of mind, feelings, traits of character, plans, purposes, intentions, or other perquisites of autonomous man really are in order to get on with a scientific analysis of behavior. (Skinner, 1971b, p. 16)

> The difficulty is that almost all of what is called behavioral science continues to trace behavior to states of mind, feelings, traits of character, human nature, and so on. Physics and biology once followed similar practices and advanced only when they discarded them. (Skinner, 1971b, p. 24)

This line of thought represents a blurring of epistemological and ontological lines. Skinner attributes the failure of the behavioral sciences to the out-of-date belief that a specialized entity (a self) is the possessor of knowledge, a personalized vessel to be filled as one learns. Skinner wants to erase this overlapping quality of being and knowing. By making knowledge the sole province of the method of natural science, the need for a self is eliminated. When knowledge is conceived of solely as a product of science and contingencies, then all control and responsibility is shifted from an autonomous person to the observable environment.

> A self is a repertoire of behavior appropriate to a given set of contingencies. The identity conferred upon a self arises from the contingencies responsible for the behavior. (Skinner, 1971b, p. 199)

To Skinner, the idea that a person learns or gains knowledge is preposterous. In actuality, what really occurs is that an organism gains a repertoire of behavior as a result of environmental contingencies. This organism can "know" only those parts of reality that can be gleaned through the methods of scientific empiricism. This belief is a central issue in Skinner's epistemological ideas.

Skinner deplores the metaphysical generalizations that have pervaded the behavioral sciences from their beginnings. He feels that most of these generalizations of cosmic proportions are either nonexistent or even if they do exist, they are not important. Any behavioral science, if it is to succeed, must devote itself to a high degree of specificity, and this sought-after degree of specificity is most readily available through modern empirical technology. Skinner believed

> advances in the experimental analysis of behavior suggest that for the first time we can develop a true technology of education [learning]. This technology, following the practice of the laboratory, will use instrumentation to equip students with large repertoires of verbal and nonverbal behavior. Even more important, the instrumentation will be able to nurture enthusiasm for continued study... The major components of this educational technology taken from experimental psychology include, in addition to the instrumentation, an assumption that the behaviors to be established are operants which must be gradually shaped through the application of experimental methodology. (Staats & Staats, 1963, p. 416)

In this manner, a certain type of behavior (learning) is acquired according to operant conditioning principles. Reinforcements are then necessary to the maintenance and acquisition of learning. "Furthermore, following upon a stimulus-response approach, the attempt has been to break the complex behaviors into simpler components" (Staats & Staats, 1963, p. 417). This idea reflects a long-standing antimetaphysical-environmental belief that the knowledge available to humans is best achieved by continually breaking a subject down into simpler parts until one arrives at the "thing" itself. Behavior is only understood when one reduces it to its most fundamental level and totally understands that simple part and uses it to build on, thus advancing from particular to more generalized understandings. Skinner denies that such a step-by-step technological investigation of humanity and the process of knowledge in any way mechanizes environmental thought. "Man is not made into a machine by analyzing his behavior [including learning] in mechanical terms" (Skinner, 1971b, p. 202). But even in denying the mechanistic overtones of environmentalism, Skinner cannot completely get away from the analogy. "Man is a machine in the sense that he is a complex system behaving in lawful [according to natural law] ways, but the complexity is extraordinary" (Skinner, 1971b, p. 202). "A scientific analysis of behavior dispossesses autonomous man and turns the control he has been said to exert over to the environment" (Skinner, 1971b, p. 205).

In summary, it is easy to see that environmental epistemology, especially as interpreted by Skinner, largely follows the guidelines for knowledge laid down by the antimetaphysical tradition. The emphasis is on empiricism and breaking a "whole" down into its component parts for purposes of analysis. There is a marked pragmatic outlook in environmental beliefs and also a tendency to deny absolutes and concentrate on relative experiences. Also, Skinner's interpretation of environmental thought places heavy emphasis on conditioning principles, environmental contingencies, and the belief that all knowledge resides in the sciences. It would seem that the epistemological defining criteria of Skinner's beliefs, environmentalism, and antimetaphysics overlap on almost every fundamental point.

In dealing with axiological issues, environmental thought probably rests on a less firm foundation than its ontological and epistemological principles. Arbuckle (1958) has often dealt with the complexity of human values in a counseling setting. It is the very nature of this complexity that causes environmentalism to encounter more diversity within its ranks when the central issue is personal, ethical, and religious values. These issues are clearly less amenable to the empirical methodology adopted by environmentalism. Skinner is, to his credit, one of those environmentalists who remains consistent in the face of the complexity of human values, and he continues to examine axiological issues mainly in the light of the same environmental-antimetaphysical position employed to explain ontological and epistemological principles.

To a great degree Skinner simply extends the epistemological beliefs of environmentalism to include axiological concerns also. Values are a set of behaviors that one acquires exactly like all other forms of learned behaviors. They are based on contingencies of reinforcement. Skinner sees no reason for maintaining a special niche in a science of human behavior for values. He claimed that there were only two ways to examine this issue.

> In what we may call the prescientific view, a person's behavior is at least to some extent his own achievement. He is free to deliberate, decide, and act, possibly in original ways and he is to be given credit for his successes and blamed for his failures. In the scientific view, a person's behavior is determined by a genetic endowment traceable to the evolutionary history of the species and by the environmental circumstances to which as an individual he has been exposed. (Skinner, 1971b, p. 101)

Skinner admits that neither of these opposing views can be positively proved, but he definitely believes that the weight of evidence strongly indicates the correctness of the "scientific" view. This view sees value in exactly the same context as all other human behaviors. They are overt actions that are reinforced and become a part of a behavioral repertoire or are actions which are not reinforced (except negatively) and thus fail to become a part of a behavioral repertoire.

> When we say that a value judgment is a matter not of fact but of how someone feels about a fact, we are simply distinguishing between a thing and its reinforcing effect. Things themselves are studied by physics and biology, usually without reference to their value, but the reinforcing effects of things are the province of behavioral science, which, to the extent that it is concerned with operant reinforcement, is a science of values. Things are good (positively reinforcing) or bad (negatively reinforcing) because of the contingencies of survival under which the species evolved. (Skinner, 1971b, p. 104)

He totally dismisses the idea that something could be good or bad in and of itself. "To make a value judgment by calling something good or bad is to classify it in terms of its reinforcing effects" (Skinner, 1971, p. 105). In his interpretation of axiology, generalized verbal labels such as good, bad, and justice are worthless until one can establish the reinforcers that gave birth to the verbal codification of such words as good and bad

Values are not possessions of a personal self. They are learned behaviors of an organism that have been subject to certain contingencies of reinforcement. These contingencies of reinforcement are usually arranged by society and reflect an attempt to induce in its members those behaviors most likely to contribute to the survival of the society.

> In an operant analysis of the stimulus control of verbal behavior, we can identify the referent of abstract terms but terms like "morality" and "justice" raise an additional problem. It can be solved by recognizing that the behavior we call "moral" or "just" is a product of special kinds of social contingencies arranged by governments, religions, economic systems, and ethical groups. We need to analyze those contingencies if we are to build a world in which people behave morally and justly and a first step in that direction is to dismiss morality and justice as personal possessions. (Skinner, 1976, pp. 268–269)

> Man is perhaps unique in being a moral animal, but not in the sense that he possesses morality; he has constructed a social environment in which he behaves with respect to himself and others in moral ways. (Skinner, 1976, p. 263)

Terms such as justice, truth, and goodness are not absolutes. In environmental thought justice is simply that which a society decides to call just. It is not a quality that exists in itself. It, like all values, is to a certain extent "invented." A society decides what is just and reinforces it for the good of the individual and the society. Skinner stated that

> The only good things are positive reinforcers, and the only bad things are negative reinforcers. What is maximized or minimized, or what is ultimately good or bad, are things, not feelings, and men work to achieve them or to avoid them not because of the way they feel but because they are positive or negative reinforcers. (Skinner, 1971b, p. 107)

A personal system of value does not develop in a person and one does not act for the good of society because of a feeling of belongingness, nor does one refuse to act because of feelings of alienation. A so-called value system is simply and totally a product of the control exerted by the social environment. One's "feelings" play absolutely no role whatsoever (Skinner, 1971b).

> The principal technique employed in the control of the individual by any group of people who have lived together for a sufficient length of time is as follows, the behavior of the individual is classified as either "good" or "bad" or, to the same effect, "right" or "wrong" and is reinforced or punished accordingly. The behavior of an individual is usually called good or right insofar as it reinforces other members of the group and bad or wrong insofar as it is aversive. (Skinner, 1953, p. 324)

This axiological principle is a direct result of the antimetaphysical-environmental ontological belief that eliminates an essential self and places human beings wholly in the realm of the natural world. In this natural world reinforcing things happen to animals without being called good or bad. Humans have verbal behavior and they can refer to these reinforcers as good and bad but they respond to the reinforcers exactly as other animals and the rest of the natural world. "To make a value judgment by calling something good or bad is to classify it in terms of its reinforcing effects" (Skinner, 1971b, p. 105). The entire natural world operates as a result of these reinforcing effects. People can call them good and bad if they so choose, but it is really not important. "The reinforcing effect is the important thing" (Skinner, 1971b, p. 105).

The absence of a self in environmental thought opens the way for those who would criticize environmentalism for its deterministic character. Without an essential self making moral decisions and facing moral crises and making choices based on what one believes is right, the position (environmentalism) is left with a rather simple biological organism that possesses a certain set of genetic characteristics and has been acted upon by certain environmental contingencies, some positive and some aversive, and, on the face of it, this human organism is totally determined by the genetic code and the environment. Without a self making choices, being responsible, being unpredictable, and virtually unfathomable at times, environmentalism can only see humans as determined products with a value system equally determined through arranged contingencies of reinforcement. In this view a person does not "have" a value system; instead one is given a value system designed not on any basis of right, truth, goodness, beauty, and justice, but rather on the basis of expediency.

> You should tell the truth is a value judgment to the extent that it refers to reinforcing contingencies. We might translate [environmentally] it as follows: If you are reinforced by the approval of your fellow men, you will be reinforced when you tell the truth. The value is to be found in the social contingencies maintained for purposes of control. It is ethical or moral judgment only in the sense that ethos and mores refer to the customary practices of a group. (Skinner, 1971b, pp. 112–113)

Skinner is saying here that the truth, since it is relative and fluctuates from experience to experience, is not important. The only things of importance are the social contingencies maintained for purposes of control and for purposes of determining values for humankind.

> To attribute moral and ethical behavior to environmental contingencies seems to leave no room for absolutes. It suggests a kind of relativism in which what is good is what ever is called good. (Skinner, 1976, p. 216)

In turn, what is called good is that which a society decides to promulgate through reinforcement; that which is believed to be of positive benefit to that society. Axiology then becomes something of a moral democracy that tends toward the espousal of relative values that promote the general will. Skinner claims that society does not need moral people in order to prosper. In fact, he even denies the fact that people can be moral. "What is needed is a restoration of social environments in which people behave in ways called moral" (Skinner, 1976, p. 215).

> Government for the benefit of the governed is easily classified as an ethical or moral issue. This need not mean that governmental design is based upon any absolute principles of right or wrong but rather... that it is under the control of long-term consequences [reinforcers]. (Skinner, 1953, p. 244)

All these ideas strongly suggest that an axiological system is not devised by anyone. Rather, after the fact, an axiological system is codified as it evolves in terms of aiding human survival.

> Human behavior does not depend upon the prior choice of any value. When a man jumps out of the way of a car, we may say that he "chooses life rather than death." But he does not jump because he has so chosen; he jumps because jumping is evoked by certain stimulating circumstances. (Skinner, 1953, p. 432)

It is not the self-directed choosing of an individual person that occurs in the above situation. Instead it is merely an example of "behavior that usually leads to survival because the behaving individual has been selected by survival in the process of evolution" (Skinner, 1953, p. 433).

There are then no questions of "oughts" or "shoulds" that really have any validity. What really occurs is the development of certain behavior patterns as a result of certain contingencies of reinforcement and then at a later date, when the behavior has repeatedly been subject to the same reinforcement, then man, because he is verbal, places labels such as "should" and "ought" on these behaviors for the sake of convenience. If for some reason the contingencies of reinforcement were to change, then in short order the behavior would change and this would also necessitate a change in "shoulds" and "oughts." Values based on such a system are relative, utilitarian, and unintentional, at least from a personal standpoint.

> A person acts intentionally... not in the sense that he possesses an intention [to do good] which he then carries out, but in the sense that his behavior has been strengthened by consequences. (Skinner, 1971b, p. 108)

There are no "built in" values as part of the human makeup. In such a system no one can really be brave or trustworthy or honest because these are not seen as characteristics. They are simply examples of behavior. Also, behavior, when it occurs, is not the result of a responsible act or choice of the individual.

> A brave act is merely poetic shorthand for the act of a person who shows bravery by performing it. But we call a man brave because of his acts, and he behaves bravely only when environmental circumstances induce him to do so. The circumstances changed his behavior; they have not implanted a trait or a virtue. (Skinner, 1971b, p. 197)

Personal happiness can only be understood to represent those reinforcers which have contributed to survival value, and personal esteem among one's fellows is a result of the conditional reinforcers used to induce a person to behave for the good of others (Skinner, 1971b).

In the final analysis then, systems of value are seen by Skinner as a way for a society to control its members and perpetuate its survival. Individual values (truth, beauty, and other "traditional" values) are relative and are determined by a society and then verbally labeled as a way of identifying various behaviors. The labels themselves are unimportant and will vary from society to society. Often the same label, such as justice, can be used by different societies to describe two vastly different and even oppositional behaviors. But one of Skinner's main points concerning value is the idea that the labels applied to behaviors are relatively unimportant. What is important is the behavior itself and the environmental contingency that caused a particular behavior. Skinner claims that in many cases even the verbal labels are misapplied and the terms right and wrong could more accurately be referred to as manners, customs, or social mores.

> No matter how we ultimately explain the action of the group in extending the ethical classifications of "right" and "wrong" to manners or customs, we are on solid ground in observing the contingencies by virtue of which the behavior characteristic of a particular group is maintained. As each individual comes to conform to a standard pattern, he also comes to support that pattern... Moreover, his own conforming behavior contributes to the standard with which the behavior of others is compared. Once a custom, manner, or style has arisen, therefore, the social system becomes reasonably self-sustaining. (Skinner, 1953, pp. 418–419)

To Skinner, ethics, morality, and axiology itself, is merely a form of linguistic shorthand representing this process.

Just as axiology is basically an extension of the environmental-antimetaphysical position concerning epistemology, the ontological principles also form a logical extension to a philosophical position concerning the nature of God. Skinner himself is an oft-confessed atheist but, oddly enough, this is not in itself an important point. The importance of Skinner's atheism lies in its justification (on mostly ontological grounds) and how this justification represents an almost perfect continuation of the environmental-antimetaphysical argument disposing of the possibility of a supreme being or supernatural being. The fact that Skinner is an atheist is, overall, of little consequence, but the fact of his eminence in psychology, and especially environmental psychology, and the fact that the reasons behind his personal atheism so accurately parallel the antimetaphysical tradition concerning this subject is of extreme importance.

Because he has been a strong advocate for so long about the power of the environment to shape behavior, Skinner takes care to likewise give this careful consideration in examining the influences on his own life. Concerning a belief in God, Skinner admits that in his family he was taught to fear God, the police, and what others might think. He later claimed that the rigidity of his early environment might have been the spur that led him to try to prove that people do not think at all (Harris, 1971). This rigidity and the times when "grandmother Skinner had him peer into the glowing coals of the parlor stove to gain a sense of hell" (Harris, 1971, p. 34) formed extremely negative reactions that were later to harden into Skinner's adamant stand on the nonexistence of a supreme being and the harmfulness of religion in general. This idea of past actions and reactions helping to predispose one to future beliefs will be discussed in the final chapter. As previously stated, at this point this examination is more interested in Skinner's general philosophy (as it parallels past antimetaphysical thought and as it influences modern environmental thought) than in the personal details of his past life. But these personal details should not be underestimated or ignored in terms of "shaping" the eventual outcomes of Skinner's theory. It must be remembered that Skinner's single great contribution to psychology was his formulation of the principles of operant conditioning. A large part of his influence has been wrought up in his championing a certain philosophy, a way of life (the antimetaphysical-environmental position). It is strictly out of this philosophy (not his work in psychology) that Skinner's ideas of a supreme being are born.

In forming his opinions on the nature of God, Skinner logically follows the ontological principles previously examined. A path to a supernatural being begins with "the notion that in each of us there is a mentalistic being—an ego, personality, anima, spirit, character, soul, or mind that is somehow free" (Harris, 1971, p. 33). Skinner's ontological denial of this autonomous part of humanity logically necessitates the denial of any form of supernaturalism to serve as the sponsor of this autonomy.

> To take its place, Skinner offers the passionless hypothesis of his experimental laboratory: each man and woman is a unique bundle of behaviors determined by environment; only that, and nothing more. Through evolution the environment selected the behaviors that survive in our genes, and environmental conditioning shapes each of us in this life. (Harris, 1971, p. 33)

No form of Deity is or need be involved in this process. Earlier in human history, forms of supernaturalism were necessary to explain things that seemingly were inexplicable.

> Man's first experience with causes probably came from his own behavior: things moved because he moved them. If other things moved, it was because someone else was moving them, and if the mover could not be seen, it was because he was invisible. Gods and demons served in this way as the causes of physical phenomena. (Skinner, 1971a, p. 38)

Skinner (1971a) claimed that biology and physics have progressed beyond these superstitions but many of the behavioral sciences still insist on attributing behavior to something "in" man "and almost everyone attributes human behavior to intentions, purposes, aims, and goals" (Skinner, 1971b, p. 8).

Skinner believes that it is modern science that will eventually deliver humanity from its penchant for superstition. All gods of the great religions have in common a sense of wonder, awe, fear, and mystery. Skinner is very clear when he says that "its [science's] goal is the destruction of mystery" (Skinner, 1971a, p. 58). As science erases more and more of the mysterious and reveals events to be totally rational and natural examples of causes and effects, it rids the world of more and more superstition. This, to Skinner, is a valuable aim, and will, in the long run, aid humankind's survival. Human behavior is heavily superstitious and most of these behaviors are strengthened by "accidental" contingencies that develop into the ritualistic practices that mark humanity's obsession with the idea of a supernatural overseer. "Superstitious rituals in human society usually involve verbal formulae and are transmitted as part of the culture" (Skinner, 1953, p. 87). Much of this is sheer cultural habit with only occasional justificatory contingencies, i.e., miracles, to sustain the process. Skinner admits that beliefs in a supernatural entity are so entrenched in human societies that people fail to see the natural causes of natural phenomena as revealed through the physical senses. Instead, people refer to absolutes, prime movers, and final causes. Science is the only way to overcome such superstition, and Skinner devotes much of his energies to promulgating just this point of view. He claimed (1953) that it was a fundamental principle of science that ruled out all final causes; all nonnatural explanations for phenomena or events. Statements alluding to purposes, incentives, or goals in reference to a supernatural entity are exactly like the statements of purposes, incentives, or goals when directed to humankind. Such ideas "are usually reducible to statements about operant conditioning, and only a slight change is required to bring them within the framework of a natural science" (Skinner, 1953, p. 87).

The key points involved in Skinner's dismissal of any idea of a supreme being are these: his ontological belief that the natural world is all there is and humans take their place (with no a priori or essential characteristics) wholly within this natural world, and his epistemological belief that this world is best revealed through natural science and the physical senses. Human beings are a product of relative experiential contingencies and biology and they have no special or absolute knowledge of either themselves or their world. Axiologically humans are

> within the framework of a natural science and certain kinds of behavior are observed when people live together in groups, kinds of behavior which are directed toward the control of the individual and which operate for the advantage of other members of the group. We define "good" and "bad," or "right" and "wrong" with respect to a particular set of practices. We account for the practices and the effects which they have on the individual and in turn on the group. (Skinner, 1953, p. 328)
>
> Such a criterion as the "greatest good of the greatest number" represents a type of explanation, based upon the principle of maxima and minima, which has often proved useful in the physical sciences. (Skinner, 1953, p. 329)

These foundational principles necessitate a natural cause and a natural explanation of all phenomena, events, and behaviors. Since obviously there can be no natural cause or explanation for a supernatural being, it logically follows then that no such being can exist. This is the position adopted by Skinner in his work and in his philosophy of life. His position serves as a perfect example of the foundational principles concerning the existence of a supreme being in the antimetaphysical-environmental school of thought.

This line of antitheological thought is much opposed on many sides, but Skinner holds fast to the idea that deliverance from such theological "problems" will propel humanity to a new dawn of enlightenment. There are those who claim that it is Skinner's plan to get rid of both "man" and God as we now know them. If by man one means "autonomous man" and by God one means a supernatural overseer, then Skinner cheerfully admits that he is indeed trying to dispose of such concepts and that all humanity will be the benefactor if he succeeds. By getting rid of autonomous man and a more than natural God "we can turn to the real causes of human behavior—from the inferred to the observed, from the miraculous to the natural, from the inaccessible to the manipulable" (Skinner, 1971b, p. 201). The humanists lean heavily on Hamlet's interpretation of human beings, "how like a God," but Pavlov, the environmental scientist, was, to Skinner, more accurate and more helpful when he paraphrased Hamlet's credo concerning humanity to "how like a dog." Regardless of the resistance with which such a statement is usually greeted, Skinner believed

> that it was a step forward. A god is the archetypal pattern of explanatory fiction, of a miracle working, of the metaphysical. Man is much more than a dog, but like a dog he is within range of a scientific analysis. (Skinner, 1971a, p. 78)

The abolition of these superstitions is a process that Skinner feels is long overdue. He (1971a) saw it (superstition) as a device to explain what cannot be explained in any other way. All superstition has been constructed in ignorance, and as understanding increases, the very stuff of which it is composed vanishes. A particular practice may be superstitiously recommended because it maximizes some such entity as salvation or the glory of God. Such justifications, though, are presumably beyond the realm of science, but an analysis of techniques permits one to account for the behavior of the controller and controllee without raising the question of any ultimate effect of this sort. In short, a supernatural being, a God, is not necessary in humanity's present or future, and the belief in such a being has often hindered humankind's past attempts at progress. A God of this type is beyond relative experiential events, beyond the natural world, beyond the bounds of science and objective verification, and therefore, to Skinner, beyond belief.

Chapter V

Viktor Frankl

In the previous chapter, the works of B. F. Skinner were examined with the intent to try to isolate the fundamental principles inherent in his writings and relate these principles to their natural ideological ancestry. Just as Skinner represents the antimetaphysical-environmental thread running throughout this study, Viktor Frankl represents the opposing metaphysical-humanist thread existing throughout this text. Earlier, when the major underlying philosophical foundations for the humanist position were being identified, it was noted that on every major topic, ontology, epistemology, and axiology, the school of thought known as existentialism differed in some way with the mainstream of other humanistic thought. Since Frankl is almost always identified with existentialism perhaps one might think him a poor choice to represent the theoretical mainstream of humanism. A study of his works, though, simply does not lead to this conclusion. In many ways, especially with regard to ontological principles, Frankl reveals a sense of phenomenology much more in tune with the humanist movement than with his "fellow" existentialists. On the traditional essence versus existence question that often separates the existentialists from other humanists, Frankl simply refuses to let one rule out the other. He profoundly believes that a person defines his/her existence as he/she experiences it, but he just as strongly ascribes to the idea that humans are special because of an innate, essential nature. Frankl refers to this essential nature as the spiritual domain (he also often uses the term self) and claims that humanity is what it is specifically because of this domain.

> Each human being is unique in both his essence (Sasein) and his existence (Dasein) and thus is neither expendable nor replaceable. In other words, he is a particular individual with his unique personal characteristics who experiences a unique historical context in a world which has special opportunities and obligations reserved for him alone. (Frankl, 1967, p. 44)

"Man is more than psyche: Man is spirit" (Frankl, 1967, p. 63). Frankl held that a human is more than a biologic, conditioned entity. "A human being is not one thing among others: Things are determining each other, but man is self-determining" (Frankl, 1967, p. 63). In these words, one can see that Frankl is very much in tune with the fundamental principles of humanism previously identified. Over all, Frankl's works provide an excellent counterpoint for the position embraced by Skinner as examined in the preceding chapter.

The heart of Frankl's ontological position is very well outlined in the above quotes. Whereas Skinner frequently states that most of humankind's troubles begin when they turn away from the objective and the impersonal, Frankl eschews this idea as nonsense and instead paints a portrait of humanity that is both subject as well as object-oriented and a humanity that most importantly is highly personalized. To be sure, humans are greatly influenced by the biologic genetic code that helps to shape their being. Equally, there is no doubt that a particular environment is a powerful determining force in one's life. It is at this ontological point that environmentalism stops, but Frankl and the humanists see this as only part of the make-up of a human being. In addition, there is a decision-making, conscious self that is aware of both the world and its own unique self-hood. It is this dimension (Frankl chooses to call this the spiritual domain) that makes man special over and above naturalistic and objective concerns. He (1975) argued that those past philosophies and psychotherapies which have been atomistic, reductionistic, mechanistic, and deterministic have reduced man to either the level of the instinctual animal or the shaped machine. Frankl concentrates instead

> on the autonomy of spiritual existence. Spiritual is...used without any religious connotation...just to indicate that we are dealing with a specifically human phenomenon (in contrast to the subhuman phenomena that we share with other animals). In other words, the "spiritual" is what is human in man. (Frankl, 1975, p. 23)

Authentic existence (being) is present where a self is making decisions, not where an id is driving and not where an environment is shaping that self (Frankl, 1975). This idea of self is most important, and Frankl's entire counseling strategy, and indeed, his entire philosophy of life, hinges on this belief. Frankl cautions that the idea is so important that one must not think in terms of "having" a self. As Frankl put it (1975), "I do not 'have' a self, but I 'am' a self" (p. 28). By choosing these semantical arguments, Frankl makes it clear that this dimension of self is, in the hierarchy of ontology, the highest form of being. One's biologic nature cannot be denied, nor can one's environmental status. But both these forms of being are secondary to the self, and it is the self that makes humans what they are. Frankl (1973) reminded us that in the original German the term self was translated from "geist which means the core or nucleus of the personality" (p. 9).

Frankl's principle of a conscious self implies a free, self-determining entity built on the ground of the choices one makes. To be human, one must be conscious and to be conscious means to make decisions, and decisions make a life full of consequences that result from our innate ability to choose.

> There is no reason to suppose that self-consciousness, the recognition of a creature by itself as a "self," can exist except in contrast with an "other," a something which is not the self. It is against an environment, and preferably a social environment, an environment of other selves, that the awareness of *Myself* sinks in... A creature with no environment would have no choices to make: so that freedom, like self-consciousness (if they are not, indeed the same thing) demands the presence to the self of something other than the self. (Lewis, 1973, p. 17)

This idea of responsibility is the reverse side of the principle of an autonomous self. It is this responsibility that implies a sense of obligation and meaning in Frankl's ontological scheme (Frankl, 1973). This sense of obligation and meaning is totally absent in all other organic and inorganic planes of existence save for humankind alone. Frankl (1973) credited humanistic (metaphysical) modes of thought

> the honor of having shown that the existence of man is essentially concrete and subjective... For the presentation of human life as singular and unique is an implicit summons to men to actualize in their own lives these unique and singular possibilities. (p. 55)

It is only human beings who have this freedom. But Frankl continually cautioned (1973) "that human freedom is not a 'freedom from' but a 'freedom to' a freedom to accept with responsibility" (Frankl, 1973, p. 52). Frankl states that of the major psychotherapies, only humanism presents humans with this type of being. Freudian thought makes humans totally free, but because of the belief in instinctive drives it allows this freedom without the "burden" of responsibility for one's actions. Environmental thought deprives humans of both their freedom to choose and the responsibility of those choices. Only in humanism is a person both free and responsible for that freedom. In only this way can being have meaning. Humans have the essential, innate potential for meaning, but only through existence, in the building of one's life through one's choices is this meaning discovered in being. "Meaning sets the pace for being. Existence falters unless it is lived in terms of transcendence toward something beyond itself" (Frankl, 1967, p. 12).

> Once meaning orientation turns into meaning confrontation, that stage of maturation and development is reached in which freedom... becomes responsibleness. Man is responsible for the fulfillment of the specific meaning of his personal life. But he is also responsible before something or to something, be it society, or humanity or mankind, or his own conscience. There is a significant number of people who interpret their own existence not just in terms of being responsible to some "thing" but rather to some "one," namely, to God... In any case, responsibleness is the very essence of human existence. (Frankl, 1967, pp. 12–13)

In his works Frankl deals little with the humanistic idea of absolutes in terms of being human. This defining criteria is dealt with in more depth, as will be seen, in Frankl's ideas about knowing, valuing, and God. In terms of humanity and existence, Frankl chooses to follow the more strict existentialist line and usually deals with humans in their finiteness. In fact, he is convinced that it is just this finite nature of being (at least in this world) that gives meaning to a person's actions and choices.

> How often we hear the argument that death does away with the meaning of life altogether. That in the end all man's works are meaningless, since death ultimately destroys them. Now, does death really decrease the meaningfulness of life? On the contrary. For what would our lives be like if they were not finite in time, but infinite? If we were immortal, we could legitimately postpone ever acting forever... But in the face of death as absolute finis to our future and boundary to our possibilities, we are under the imperative of utilizing our lifetimes to the utmost, not letting the singular opportunities—whose finite sum constitutes the whole of life—pass by unused. (Frankl, 1973, pp. 63–64)

But despite this existential "policy line," Frankl does, at least implicitly, refer to absolutes in terms of being. He often talks about what he refers to as "the supra-meaning" in a human life. "This ultimate [absolute] meaning necessarily exceeds and surpasses the finite intellectual capacities of man:... we speak, in this context of a supra-meaning" (Frankl, 1959, p. 187). The fact that many existentialists teach that life is meaningless and the fact that the so-called environmental viewpoint teaches that Frankl's supra-meaning is nonverifiable and nonrational in no way proves that such ultimate qualities do not exist. In fact, in Frankl's opinion, it is one of life's great paradoxes that one must learn to "bear his incapacity to grasp its unconditional [ultimate] meaningfulness in rational terms" (Frankl, 1959, p. 188).

In dealing with this absolutist point, Frankl liked to use the example of his questioning a group of students and clinicians about an experiment in which, in order to speed the development of a polio serum, an ape was experimentally and quite painfully punctured with a needle again and again. Frankl asked the group if the ape could grasp the meaning of its suffering. Without fail everyone felt that with its limited intelligence the ape could not enter the world of human nature which was the only world in which its suffering would be understandable or have meaning (Frankl, 1973). Frankl then pursued the logical point to his story by asking,

> And what about man? Are you so sure that the human world is a terminal point in the evolution of the cosmos? Is it not conceivable that there is still another dimension possible, a world beyond man's world; a world in which the question of an ultimate meaning of human suffering [and being] would find an answer? (Frankl, 1959, p. 187)

Frankl never tires of saying that the only really transitory or relative aspects of being are the potentialities one faces in one's choices. The minute these potentialities are acted upon they are rendered absolute realities and it is to this absolute idea that a person, as a self-directed self, is responsible.

As a representative theorist for humanistic thought, Frankl's works cover all the major ontological points of the humanistic-metaphysical point of view. Humankind is subject as well as object and if a ranking has to be decided upon then the subjective must outweigh the objective. Frankl deals with the idea of a unique, free, responsible, self-determining self that exists in a different dimension than humans as animals only, or humans as products of environmental conditioning only. Finally, Frankl views humanity as more than existing relatively and merely reacting experience by experience. Instead, humans can plan, they can choose, and not only can they react, most importantly humans can act!

In terms of epistemology, Frankl's writings reveal his beliefs in a very straight-forward fashion. Admittedly, Frankl does not devote a great bulk of his work to epistemological musings, but what he does have to say on the subject is very clear and not open to misinterpretation or misunderstanding.

In the book *Psychotherapy and Existentialism: Selected Papers on Logotherapy* (1967), Frankl made a very key statement linking humanistic counseling thought to the defining criteria of the metaphysical movement. This similarity concerns the idea of the existence of certain absolutes; in the case of epistemology he was referring to absolute truth.

> I personally doubt whether... truth can ever be distinguished from untruth by evidence which is universally acceptable to man... It is not possible, either, to declare [prove] that any one of them [claims for truth] is superior to the others. Similarly, no language can justifiably be called "true" or "false," but through each of these truths—*the one truth*—may be approached as if from different sides, and through each language it is also possible to err, and even to lie. (p. 13)

Frankl is saying that even though many may recognize degrees of truth or situational truths (that which may be true in one particular moment of existence and false in another) he believes that these "truths" only have meaning when compared to universal truth. Frankl doubts humanity's ability to objectively prove such truth, but he does not at all doubt the existence of that truth. The various degrees of truth recognized by humans are comparative reference points in relation to that which is ultimately true. Though the proof of such truth may lie outside one's objective or scientific capacities, the truth itself is "knowable" through the specialized and subjective nature of the human self and the relationship of this self with the ultimate nature of the cosmos. Frankl (1967) wrote that the search for truth itself was based on subjective grounds but it also implied a certain amount of objectivity. Truth is not something that we simply attach or attribute meanings to, nor do we merely invent it to explain a certain phenomena. Truth is detected, usually by those making an effort to do so, not invented. But because of finite qualities, humankind often fails to detect the truth. This says a great deal about the nature of human beings in this life, but it says nothing about the quality of the truth itself. The truth exists whether or not humanity succeeds in the effort to discern it. Its existence depends on its own absolute quality, not on humanity's ability to invent or reveal it. Frankl (1967) conceived of each human being in the usual existential manner stating that each life is unique and totally singular. But in a way that deviates somewhat from the existential norm, he sees humanity's uniqueness in terms of a backdrop of ultimacy.

A human life may be individuated but in spite of this quality, life itself persists in asking the same old questions of each individual.

> Life is a chain of questions which man has had to answer by answering for life, to which he has to respond by being responsible, by making decisions, by deciding which answer to give to the individual questions. And I venture to say that each question has only one answer—the right one! (Frankl, 1967, p. 17)

This one right answer is nothing but Frankl's way of confirming the existence of such a thing as absolute truth.

By nature of humanity's being and the specialized nature of a self, humans are committed to a search for the ultimate quality of truth. This does not necessarily imply that humans are capable of finding the truth in every instance. Humans are not exempt from error. But to Frankl, the idea of trying to always go in the direction of truth necessarily builds a positive quality into life even as humans often fail to achieve *the* truth. But in a life dedicated to pursuing the absolute qualities of truth, one gets ever closer to this achievement. Frankl, both epistemologically and axiologically, was fond of paraphrasing Goethe concerning this idea of steadily moving closer to the goal, "We must always aim at the bull's eye—although we know that we will not always hit it!" (Frankl, 1967, p. 17). Humanity must always strive to attain that which is absolutely true. Otherwise, humankind will fail to attain even that which is relatively true (Frankl, 1967).

Frankl also seems to imply a belief that perhaps any idea of ultimacy, including ultimate truth, is approached entirely on individualistic grounds. It is not discovered by one person and then distributed to others. He (1967) claimed that it was entirely the province of the conscious self to determine and search for such ultimate meanings. "Anyone's conscience, as anything human, is subject to error; but this does not release man from his obligation to obey it—existence involves the risk of error" (Frankl, 1967, p. 13). Such a world means, of course, that humans might indeed err in their search for truth, but in this kind of world the equal possibility exists that one's subjective and objective decisions might discover the very essence of "the truth." He (1967) stated that he much preferred to live in a world where humans might make errors but also might discover the truth, rather than live in a world where such a commodity as the truth is believed nonexistent and humans are thus "debased and degraded to a mere functionary of a party or the state" (p. 14). Whatever one knows or sees in this life is phenomenologically filtered through the spirit (the unique essential self) and a totally objective view is impossible. Through this phenomenological approach, the visual field is broadened and ultimate meanings and ultimate truths are perhaps ascertainable. The growing awareness of one's self reveals the fact that life never ceases to reveal meanings and truths even up to its last moments.

> This is due to the fact that, as a phenomenological analysis can show us, man not only finds his life meaningful through his deeds, his works, his creativity, but also through his experiences, his encounters with what is true, good, and beautiful in the world, and last but not least, his encounter with others, with fellow human beings and their unique qualities. (Frankl, 1967, p. 14)

In this statement Frankl makes clear his belief that there are standards such as truth, goodness, and beauty that humans can apprehend. As previously stated, the fact that humans, in the real objective world, rarely actually apprehend these ultimate qualities says a great deal more about human frailty than it does about the nature or existence of such qualities.

Frankl's belief that everything, including knowledge and truth, is perceived through a sense of self-consciousness, verifies his acceptance of the validity of subjective forms of knowing. This is a prerequisite key to the fundamental metaphysical-humanist viewpoint. Everything, regardless of how objective it may appear, is internalized and understood within a subjective framework. It is, as Frankl stated (1967), "filtered" through the consciousness of a unique, essential self. This does not refute the importance of objective knowledge. It merely asserts that subjective knowing must be allowed to take its place in any epistemological hierarchy. This is the very basis of phenomenology in general and humanism in particular. "Phenomenology, as I understand it, speaks the language of man's prereflective self-understanding [subjective] rather than interpreting a given phenomenon after preconceived patterns [objective]" (Frankl, 1967, p. 2). This allows a person, through a sense of consciousness and through subjective and objective means, to make a "personal commitment to the search for truth" (Frankl, 1975, p. 121). This empirical and nonempirical search for truth is an essential part of human life, and it is the basic principle of humanistic epistemology. If the subjective realm of this search is ignored and truth is only approached through objective means, then the quest is already doomed to failure because it eliminates the subjective quality that makes humanity unique and makes truth knowable.

In his writings, Frankl devoted more time to the subject of axiology than perhaps any other single topic. He has always been extremely concerned that the subject of right and wrong has been, in history and in counseling, greatly misunderstood. His literary efforts in great part represent an attempt to present and make the case for a humanistic evaluation of morality. This evaluation follows logically from his ontological and epistemological principles previously examined. For instance, the ontological principle of the autonomy of a conscious self in decision making insures that logically this autonomous self must be held accountable for those decisions. A conscious being necessitates the position of free choice and negates the position of determinism. It also entails the subsequent state of affairs whereby one is responsible for the effects of one's choices. Stated in its simplest form, this means that from the humanistic-metaphysical point of view, one has the ability to exercise free, self-determining choices and is personally responsible for those choices. The choices themselves form the subject of axiology because invariably the choices, shorn of all the verbiage and complexities, are essentially questions of right and wrong, morality or immorality.

Though this ontological premise leading to the humanist viewpoint on value seems simple enough, it has, according to Frankl, been clouded recently (historically speaking) by antimetaphysical-environmental epistemological dialogue. Recent trends in educational thought seem to be content with simply transmitting traditions and objective knowledge, rather than presenting opportunities to refine humankind's innate capacities to find unique universal meanings and universal values. The sense of emptiness and meaninglessness that results from such teaching is reinforced by the way in which scientific findings are presented in reductionistic ways and people are indoctrinated along the lines of a mechanistic theory of humanity and a relativistic philosophy of life and morality. These modern trends in educational thought can easily be seen in both the ideational and substantive patterns in recent educational policy.

> That is, the impact of democratic institutions and growing technologies has been accompanied by new exponents in the theory of knowledge [and value] underlying learning. This change can be noted in two ways, first in the rise of positivism and second in the development of pragmatism... By adopting positivistic criteria of knowledge [in education], one necessarily inclines himself more and more toward a material world of social and physical forces. This emphasis opens the door to utilitarianism, making positivism but a prelude to

> pragmatism... This transforms the role of knowledge [and school] from making man more perfect to making him more comfortable. (Brubacher, 1965, pp. 120–121)

Such an approach toward humanity tends to make human life small and unimportant, just one thing in a natural universe of many other equal things. Frankl feels that humans are more than things and that it is their ability to choose right and wrong, which, in effect, removes them from simple "thingdom" and makes them special. Similar metaphysical-humanistic educational and moral assumptions

> make it possible to hold the line for general ... education. One leading assumption here holds that knowledge [and value] is not only unitary but absolute and universal. (Brubacher, 1965, p. 115)

"Education implies teaching. Teaching implies knowledge. Knowledge is truth. The Truth is everywhere the same" (Hutchins, 1936, pp. 96–97). The importance of this epistemological and axiological difference logically stemming from metaphysical ontological principles cannot be overstated. As William I. Thompson said, "humans are not objects that exist as chairs or tables; they live, and if they find that their lives are reduced to the mere existence of chairs and tables, they commit suicide" (cited in Frankl, 1969, p. 85). To Frankl, this is not an over dramatization. As humans create their lives through the choices they make, they are constantly behaving in a way which creates a hierarchy of values in life. In essence, a person makes one choice rather than another because it has more value to that individual. "Valuing means preferring a higher value to a lower one" (Frankl, 1969, p. 119). Each person exhibits this process of valuing through the choices and decisions made in everyday life.

Frankl finds it impossible to define human value in any other but these comparative terms. No humans, regardless of how empirically they see themselves, make choices or decisions or form beliefs on the basis of random selection. No one sees every choice as having equal value. Rather, every person makes decisions and forms beliefs on the simple basis of perceiving one choice or one belief as having more value than other existing choices or beliefs. This comparative nature applies to all types of values and beliefs. Frankl himself stated that all beliefs and values fit in one of three categories.

> I have classified them [types of values and beliefs] in terms of creative, experiential, and attitudinal values. This reflects

> the three principal ways in which man can find meaning in life. The first is what he gives to the world in terms of creation [this includes results of overt choices]; the second is what he takes from the world in terms of encounters and experiences; and the third is the stand he takes to his predicament in case he must face a fate which he cannot change [both the second and third type include a nonobserved internalized set of beliefs]. This is why life never ceases to hold a meaning, for even a person who is deprived of both creative and experiential values is still challenged by a meaning to fulfill, that is, by the meaning inherent in the right. (Frankl, 1969, p. 70)

Humanism in general and Frankl in particular have never underestimated the power of the biological and environmental constraints that are superimposed on human beings. But within these constraints one can usually exercise choices that represent a selection of what is the better course to follow, i.e., that which has more value. But even faced with a fate whose constraints are so severe that one cannot exercise creative or experiential values, one can still form attitudes and beliefs and can reap the benefits of choosing those that create meaning in life. These choices represent what Frankl calls the selection of those values that are "right." This last type of value exists because humans are unique in that they have unique selves that can objectively and subjectively judge choices and beliefs and can recognize (though often they do not) those that are better than others, and ultimately, those that are best.

Although each self is unique,

> we must not forget that...there are also situations which have something in common, and consequently there are also meanings which are shared by human beings across society and, even more, throughout history. Rather than being related to unique situations these meanings refer to the human condition. And these meanings are what is understood by values. So one may define values as those meaning universals which crystallize in the typical situations a society or even humanity has to face. (Frankl, 1969, pp. 55–56)

This clearly shows that Frankl closely follows the metaphysical-humanistic tradition of absolutes in which a value system is arranged in a hierarchy ranging from worst to best. Values are ranked in a comparative fashion and "the experience of one value includes the experience that it ranks higher than another" (Frankl, 1967, p. 57). Followed logically, this idea of comparative values and a hierarchy of values must of necessity lead one to the idea of a system of absolute values on which all others are founded and to which all others are compared. From a humanistic standpoint a "good" cannot exist without a standard, a "best," to which it can be compared. This argument, followed to its conclusion, leads to what St. Thomas often referred to as the highest good—God. This point will be dealt with in greater detail in the next section. But the axiological point of humanism to be made here clearly reflects a metaphysical heritage in that the goal to be achieved, both in society and in each unique self, is perfection. This idealistic axiological birthright is older than Plato but is also at the vanguard of counseling's "third force." In a book addressing the topic of metaphysics, J. Donald Butler (1951) identified the highest good from a metaphysical perspective as "the perfection of the self, or self-realization. Perfectionism may also have its social frame of reference" (p. 53). Humanistic texts are replete with the idea of "self-realization," meaning, in the metaphysical sense, a drive toward self-perfection. Humanistic counseling's adherence to the metaphysical tradition is made perfectly clear on this axiological point.

This gradual movement toward perfection or self-realization (or self-actualization as the term is often applied in modern counseling usage) is based on two premises: one, that humans must have some idea, some notion, of the qualities of that which is perfect and the capability to recognize it; two, humans must possess some mechanism to employ this innate recognition of that which is perfect in day to day life. Frankl believes that it is one's spiritual dimension, the conscious self, that makes humans unique in this ability to see and move toward perfection. "Conscience could be defined as the intuitive capacity of man to find out the meaning of a situation. Conscience also has the power to discover unique meanings that contradict accepted values" (Frankl, 1969, p. 63). It is this capacity for consciousness that makes humanity responsible for giving the "right" answers to life's questions and for finding the "true" meaning in a given situation (Frankl, 1969). This belief brings us back to Goethe's idea that a bull's eye is a standard. It is something to shoot for even though we know that we will not hit it every time. But to Frankl the notion of always attempting to hit the bull's eye (to be perfect) insures that as our life passes we will get ever closer to that standard. "We have to try to reach for the absolute best—otherwise we shall not even reach the relatively good" (Frankl, 1967, p. 17).

These thoughts of self-actualization and perfection permeate the metaphysical-humanistic position and represent a foundational point of the movement. The idea can be seen across the centuries. Plato (1872) taught that there was a standard of behavior (perfection) toward which everyone should strive, even though some were perhaps more capable of achieving this standard. Kant (1938) based his ideas of a transcendent afterlife on the premise that all people had an inborn drive (consciousness) to move toward perfection. Since, according to Kant, it is impossible to achieve this goal in a human lifetime, this inborn drive could reach its point of culmination only in some type of afterlife. Otherwise, life would merely represent some kind of cosmic joke; to be born with a drive that is impossible to fulfill. Modern humanistic counseling thought is formed in this same metaphysical framework of perfection.

> Human beings strive for self-actualization, which is the tendency to become all that they are capable of becoming. All individuals have an inborn urge to become a person; that is, they have the tendency toward developing...and striving for the full actualization of their potentials. (Corey, 1977, p. 49)

Thus it is as Patterson (1980) observed that "fundamentally, any man can, even under [extreme] circumstances, decide what shall become of him—mentally and spiritually" (p. 539).

In other words, through a sense of consciousness, singularly a possession of humanity, one can evaluate situations and recognize varying degrees of value. Humans can, if they so choose, recognize that which is best and can, through their exercise of free choice, move in that direction. An absolute standard exists and intuitively humans know how to recognize this standard and proceed along a path designed to lead to that culminating point. Whether or not a person heeds this intuitive drive (a "drive" according to Kant or a "sense of longing" according to Frankl) depends entirely on the individual person. Any philosophy of life or any counseling strategy that does not focus on the meanings and values of consciousness robs people of that which makes them human. An idea of life or a counseling viewpoint that is blind to value (for there is no such thing as a life or a counseling strategy that is unconcerned with value) such an idea mistakenly steals the single quality of human beings that make them unique (Frankl, 1973). It is, in the final analysis, the possession of a conscious, innate sense of self, or as Frankl puts it, a spirit, that gives rise to value or morality. This self is innately endowed with the ability to recognize that which is beautiful, that which is true, and that which is good. The denial of this self puts humanity in a position in which

> he loses the feeling of being an individual, a being with a mind, with inner freedom and personal value. He thinks of himself

> then as only a part of an enormous mass of people; his existence descends to the level of animal life. (Frankl, 1975, p. 79)

In a previous section which examined the general ontological, epistemological, and axiological foundational points of humanism, it was asserted that these points formed a logical path to the necessity of a supreme and supernatural Being. A brief review of these points seems advisable before beginning to examine Frankl's individual thoughts concerning this subject. Ontologically, a conscious self capable of at least partially understanding reality as a whole seems to logically lead to the idea that this generalized nature of reality be in some way like a conscious self—else how could a human conscious self comprehend it. Epistemologically, the world appears to have meaning that the human self can understand. From whence comes this meaning except as part of an investiture from a self that is in tune to human selves? How would one recognize truth without comparing it to that which is ultimately and absolutely true? Axiologically, the question is, how can comparative values exist (and they do indeed seem to exist), values labeled good, or better, unless a standard "best" exists to make such comparisons possible? These general points of being, knowing, and valuing logically lead one, both implicitly and explicitly, to a consistent position for the idea of God in a metaphysical-humanist framework. Humanists claim that this line of logic is as follows: God is a real being whose make up is in some fashion like the make up of a human self or spirit and from whom all reality is defined; God is the absolute truth, the end point of comparison of all knowledge and the source of all other knowledge; God is perfect, the end point of comparison of all values—the "best." This is the logical point of conclusion that metaphysical and humanistic ontology, epistemology, and axiology achieves. As stated earlier, this tends to break down when applied to individual philosophers or counseling theorists. It is most accurate at the level of the abstract foundational principles of the movement. Despite this fact, it is a worthwhile effort to examine this issue through the works of one particular humanist just as was done earlier with one particular environmentalist.

Frankl labels his own special brand of humanistic counseling as Logotherapy and he says that basically it was designed to deal not so much with biological or even psychological problems, but rather with spiritual problems, problems of that conscious and unique self of the distinctly human community. As might be imagined, Frankl has always found it difficult to refer to this spiritual dimension of humans without also raising the issue of God. He has also been at great pain in his lectures and writings to insist that his counseling method would work regardless of a subject's acceptance or rejection of a God. Despite this declaration, though, Frankl freely admits that the spirit of humanity and the relation to a greater Spirit is not just probable but unavoidable in one way or another.

> The main thesis propounded in the lecture entitled "The Unconscious God" remains still valid and tenable There is, in fact, a religious sense deeply rooted in each and every man's unconscious depths. (Frankl, 1975, p. 10)

Logotherapy was basically designed to treat problems emanating from this area of spiritual unconsciousness. "This unconscious religiousness, revealed by our phenomenological analysis, is to be understood as a latent relation to transcendence inherent in man" (Frankl, 1975, p. 61).

> This concept means no more or less than that man has always stood in an intentional relation to transcendence, even if only on an unconscious level. If one calls the intention referent of such an unconscious relation "God," it is apt to speak of an "unconscious God." This, however, in no way implies that God is unconscious to himself, but rather that God may be unconscious to man and that man's relation to God may be uncon-scious. (Frankl, 1975, pp. 61–62)

Frankl noted that in one's relation to God a person may be unconscious, but this also carries a converse point. The relationship may also be on a very conscious level. It depends entirely on the individual person. But conscious or not, he is saying that humanity does indeed have a relationship with a transcendent Being, usually referred to as God, and that even if on the unconscious level, this relationship is special and it concerns that special part of humanity, a self or spirit, that separates humans from other life forms. "But above all man's unconscious relation to God is profoundly personal" (Frankl, 1975, p. 63). A conscious relationship must then be even more personal.

Frankl also finds in God the same epistemological qualities found throughout the history of the metaphysical position. This idea refers to the absolute nature of truth and to the source of this absolute knowledge. In *The Will to Meaning*, Frankl (1969) stated that, "We are certainly justified in assuming that truth is an aspect of Deity also" (p. 93). He admitted that it is difficult for man to decipher universal truth, but in identifying God "of whom truth is in turn no more than merely one aspect" (Frankl, 1969, p. 94), he identified both the end point of comparison (the final, ultimate truth) and the source of knowledge and truth for mankind. This belief coincides exactly with the defining criteria of the metaphysical and humanistic position. When he states that every question has only one right answer and every situation has only one true meaning, he is emphasizing the absolutist epistemology of the metaphysical-humanistic tradition. This absolutist ideology must have a final referent and Frankl identifies this reference point with the designation God. Ignoring this reference point obscures the truth and sets humanity in a direction that will eventually obscure the self that makes human nature special and unique.

> Religion is a human phenomenon and as a human phenomenon it must be taken earnestly. It must be taken at face value and not dismissed by being reduced to subhuman phenomena along the lines of reductionism. Taking religion seriously allows for drawing upon the spiritual resources of the patient. In this context spiritual means uniquely and truly human. (Frankl, 1969, p. 140)

In addition to an epistemology logically leading to an idea of God, Frankl also provided arguments designed to address the prohibitive pronouncements concerning God offered by the antimetaphysical and environmental schools of thought. He fully concurred with the environmental belief that God could not be either apprehended or comprehended on the sensational or purely rational level. God is not verifiable, observable, or measurable through such means. The environmentalists and antimetaphysicians believe that these methods are the only ones available, therefore no God can exist. Frankl, in keeping with his humanist-metaphysical heritage, believes that in addition to being a body and a mind, a human being is also a soul—a conscious self. The fact that God cannot be approached on physical or mental terms does not prove that He is nonexistent. It only leads to the conclusion that His Being is only approachable on the level inherent in the human conscious self and must also be somehow like that self. As Albert Einstein once said, "Mere thinking cannot reveal to us the highest purpose" (cited in Frankl, 1969, p. 144).

> I would say that the ultimate meaning, or as I prefer to call it, the supra-meaning is no longer a matter of thinking but a matter of believing. We do not catch hold of it on intellectual grounds but on existential grounds, out of our whole being, i.e, through faith. But it is my contention that faith in the ultimate meaning is preceded by trust in an ultimate being, by trust in

God. (Frankl, 1969, p. 145) Frankl (1969) echoed the feeling expressed earlier by A. E. Taylor concerning the difficulty of using language to approach the subject of God.

> The ontological difference between being and things or for that matter the dimensional difference between the ultimate being and human beings, prevents man from really speaking of God. Speaking of God implies making being into a thing. It implies reification. (Frankl, 1969, p. 146)

Even though speaking of God has enormous expressional difficulties, Frankl agrees with the metaphysical perspective of ontology which states that human nature is unique because of an innate conscious self that is tuned, however minutely, to the same key of an ultimate Being. "In other words, man cannot speak of God but he may speak to God" (Frankl, 1969, p. 146). The being of individual humans does not provide the means for explaining an ultimate Being, but it does contain the means for some rapprochement with this ultimate Being—with God. "The three stumbling blocks, authoritarianism, rationalism, and anthropomorphism, account for much of the repression in the field of religion" (Frankl, 1969, p. 149). These obstacles, though, are not proofs of God's nonexistence. They are merely the means whereby humans deny the existence of their own unique self-hood and in the process sow the seeds for the physical and psychological problems that follow such a denial.

> People who limit reality to what is tangible and visible and for this reason tend "a priori" to deny the existence of an ultimate being, also repress religious feeling. Along with those people who are too sophisticated to embrace naive concepts of religion, there are people who are too immature to overcome a primitive epistemology. They insist that God must be visible. (Frankl, 1969, p. 152)

To humanists and metaphysicians, objectivity for the sake of objectivity is a pointless pursuit, and it fails to make an acceptable case for dispensing with ultimate meaning. Frankl (1975) tried to examine the trend of the use of pure objectivity and he believed that it was the correct tool for the scientist but objectivity became useless, even harmful, if allowed to dominate not just science but all other forms of human nature.

> In our century, a deified reason and a megalomanic technology are the repressive structures to which the religious feeling is

> sacrificed. This fact explains much of the present condition of man... With special reference to technology, however, one is reminded of a dictum by Goethe: "He who possesses art and science also has religion." But today we know only too well where man would wind up if he had science and nothing beyond it: soon the only thing that would be left of all his science would be the atom bombs he possessed. (Frankl, 1975, p. 70)

Centuries earlier, the poet Robert Burns scratched a small poem on a dusty windowpane of the technological wonder of his age (the English factory) that with special wit, insight, and brevity seems to have captured the warning in Goethe's words. On the window Burns scrawled,

> We cam na here to view your wark,
> In hopes to be mair wise,
> But only, lest we gang to Hell,
> It may be nae surprise.
> (Burns, cited by Clark, 1969, p. 321)

The idea of religion or God is so intertwined with human consciousness or spirituality that it actually is one part of the defining criteria that makes humans unique. When denied or repressed, it keeps humanity from being all it could be (actualizing the full potential of each self) and somewhat warps each person's sense of well-being in both objective and subjective reality.

> Our thoughts do revolve around the apparent timelessness of a reality—around the everpresence of that reality which man's intrinsic religiousness has revealed itself to be. It is a reality in the strict sense of phenomenological empiricism. Sometimes a person's relation to transcendence is repressed [and]...the repressed transcendence shows up and makes itself noticeable as an "unrest of the heart." (Frankl, 1975, pp. 67–68)

"So what holds true for the unconscious in general is also true for unconscious religiousness in particular: repression winds up in neurosis" (Frankl, 1975, p. 68). Frankl completely believes in this idea, and in large part, his counseling theory is designed to treat the result of what happens when humankind represses a vital part of its essential nature. As Frankl (1975) stated, "once the angel in us is repressed, he turns into a demon" (p. 70). On the other hand, if the full nature of human beings, including their sense of religiousness, is given some form of expression, then humanity can proceed to grow, both individually and as a positive part of society. "An analogous by-product is religion's inestimable contribution to mental health. After all, religion provides man with a spiritual anchor, with a feeling of security such as he can find nowhere else" (Frankl, 1969, p. 144). Finally, Frankl finds no meaning in the modern use of the term secular humanism. This term tends to make human beings something of a finished product with no reason for any theistic relationship. He follows the logic of metaphysics and discovers that humanism, in its fundamental principles, is intricately and inseparably related to theism. This relatedness must be given expression if humanity is to be truly human. "In the light of logotherapy religion is a human phenomenon... and it must be taken earnestly" (Frankl, 1969, p. 104).

This relationship between humanity and ultimate qualities seems to clearly follow the logic of the metaphysical-humanist tradition. Frankl sees people as not only biological and psychological, but as spiritual also (as self-conscious selves). Each unique self can recognize truth and goodness but is free to choose whether or not to act on this recognition. Finally, he believes in an ultimate meaning or an ultimate Being—a God that the human self is in some way related to and who serves as the final point of comparison in deciding "the truth" and "the best." Frankl most assuredly feels that his theory is aware of these points, but it takes care not to thrust these ideas on anyone. To do so would negate the essential freedom of the individual self. He (1967) stated that

> psychotherapy indeed touches the realm of religion. There is common ground enough to warrant mutual rapprochement. Bridging, however, does not mean merging. The goal of psychotherapy, of psychiatry and, quite generally, of medicine, is health. The goal of religion is something different: salvation. So much for the difference in goals. The results achieved, however, are another matter. Although religion may not aim at mental health it might result in it. Psychotherapy often results in an analogous by-product; while the doctor is not, and must not be, concerned with helping the patient regain his belief in God, time and again this is just what occurs, unintended and unexpected as it is. (pp. 32–33)

The reason for this is the overlapping nature of humanity's physical, mental, and spiritual dimensions—each influences the other. Without the dimension of a conscious self, the human life is an ultimate absurdity. With this dimension, human beings can achieve ultimate meaning. "Man is only called upon to decide between the alternatives of ultimate absurdity or ultimate meaning...through the mode of existence which he chooses" (Frankl, 1967, p. 33). "Freedom and responsibility together make man a spiritual being" (Frankl, 1967, p. 121). This spirituality is constantly "struggling and striving for a higher and ultimate meaning to his existence" (Frankl, 1967, pp. 121–122). Frankl himself equates ultimate meaning with ultimate Being and states that the Being—God—precedes the meaning. This can only imply that the Being is author of the meaning. When humans leave this Being out of their lives, they also cut off much of the meaning of life.

> At first he understood himself as a creature—in the image of his creator, God. Then came the machine age and he began to see himself as a creator—in the image of his creation, the machine: 'l'homme machine,' as La Meterie puts it. (Frankl, 1967, p. 123)

This is the modern version of the "nothing but" syndrome concerning man.

> According to the three great homunculisms—biologism, psychologism, and sociologism—man was "nothing but" either an automaton of reflexes, a bundle of drives, a psychic mechanism, or simply a product of the environment. Nothing but that was left of man, whom the psalmist had called "paulo minor Angelis" and had thus placed only just below the angels. (Frankl, 1967, p. 123)

The arguments of the metaphysical-humanist position, the ontological, epistemological, and axiological premises, all logically point to the necessity of a God. Frankl closely follows these premises to the same conclusion and rejects the "nothing but" positions of environmentalism, psychoanalysis, and other theories that deny both humanity's specialized nature and the author of that nature. "The truth [is] that love is the ultimate and highest goal to which man can aspire" (Frankl, 1975, pp. 58–59). "God is love" (*Holy Bible,* lst John 4:16).

Chapter VI

Summary

In terms of basic subject matter, this text can be broken down into three major components: an examination of the fundamental principles underlying the metaphysical and antimetaphysical positions in philosophy; an examination of the fundamental principles underlying the humanistic and environmental positions of counseling theory; and an examination of the specific works of a noted humanist and environmentalist in the realm of counseling to try to identify the foundational premises of their respective theories. It would be important to examine these three basic issues in their own right because they represent major areas of influence in both the generalized history of thought and the specific history of counseling thought. But of paramount importance to this particular study is the idea that there exists a common thread running throughout these three basic issues that effectively ties these issues together to the point of logical inseparability. The thread running throughout this text is the idea that these issues are more than related. In fact, these three issues are really not three issues at all. They are one. Establishing that thought is really the point of this enterprise. This, to some, will not represent a vast addition to humanity's storehouse of knowledge, but it is an idea that the field of counseling has virtually ignored throughout its history.

Earlier, this study presented reasons trying to show why this state of affairs in counseling has existed for so long. The real point, though, is that this state of affairs still exists (though some progress has been made by Barclay, Arbuckle, and others). Counseling literature is filled with statistical studies that are designed to investigate the multi-faceted technical and procedural aspects of the field. Such studies are, of course, positive and objective measurements that enhance both the prestige and the value of counseling. Counseling cannot grow without the experimental data generated from such studies. But something of a pendulum effect exists in the history of counseling thought. In its earliest beginnings and to a certain degree all the way through its Freudian period, counseling based its methods and conclusions almost entirely on a paradigm of subjectivity. But with the advent of the industrial age, logical positivism, learning theory, and the writings of Watson, Skinner, and other environmentalists, the counseling pendulum of thought has swung almost entirely to the side of objectivity and to those "scientists" dominated by the principle of verifiability. This study has tried to examine the fundamental principles that underlie the dramatic oppositional nature of the humanistic versus environmentalistic position of the pendulum of counseling thought. Also an attempt has been made to trace the genesis of these differing fundamental principles and also to trace the effect that these differing principles have had on individual counseling theorists.

At every point in the documentation of these ideas, the common thread mentioned above dominated the investigation and wove itself logically into every major section of this work. For instance, in the first section dealing with metaphysics versus antimetaphysics it was apparent that philosophy is often generally divided along these antagonistic lines. And even though thousands of years of philosophic history be examined, one still notices the same general defining criteria for both the metaphysical and the antimetaphysical positions. These defining criteria have been dealt with at length earlier but in a most generalized fashion the antimetaphysical position is: a belief in a purely objective and natural reality revealed through sensory input; the scientific method is the only way to know anything; values are decided upon on the basis of the greatest good for the greatest number and are relative in nature; and finally, there is no possibility of the supernatural. A quick review of the most generalized metaphysical tenets reveals: a belief in a subjective reality interpreted through a unique, essential self (soul); a belief that subjective knowledge is important and all objective knowledge is first filtered through the subjectivity of a self-conscious self and knowledge can be absolute; a belief in comparative values based on an absolute value; and the belief in a supernatural quality for reality. These arguments represent only the most general beliefs of each position and it is important for the reader to understand that one position is not being intentionally advanced over another.

These principles are perhaps familiar to most philosophers but the discussion of these principles, though philosophical in nature, was aimed not at philosophers but at counselors. This is an extremely important point. The first section of the text was not meant to be a philosophical debate designed to prove one position false and the other true. Instead, the intent was to present both sides of the debate to counselors because this philosophic debate exercises great importance in the field of counseling and most counselors are unaware of this tremendous influence. This lack of awareness of philosophical foundations prevents a necessary counseling self-examination, and it leads to the situation described earlier by Arbuckle (1965) where counselors really do not understand what they are doing, or what they think they are doing. It must be understood that this work is not meant to serve as a book for philosophers about counseling. Rather, it is meant as a book for counselors about philosophy. This distinction is important because of the continuation of the thread tying this study together. For many decades (and continuing until the present) a major argument in counseling has been conducted between the so-called environmentalists and the so-called humanists. These two schools of thought are not the result of intellectual spontaneous regeneration. They are tied and thoroughly bound with the thread of commonality to the metaphysical-antimetaphysical debate previously examined. The basic defining criteria of the metaphysical and antimetaphysical positions are respectively almost identical to the principles identified as the basic defining criteria of the humanistic and environmentalistic positions. This is why examining the content of the metaphysical and antimetaphysical arguments is so important to counselors; certainly not to resolve this on-going esoteric argument, but rather to see that these same respective philosophic arguments form the foundational pillars of both schools of counseling thought. The birth of humanism is in metaphysics. Equally, the birth of environmentalism is in antimetaphysics. It is to the detriment of counseling to remain unaware or to purposefully ignore this relationship.

The attempt was made to continue the examination of this common thread into the specific area of individual counseling theorists. Examining the works of Frankl and Skinner clearly reflects the philosophical thread that dominates the field of counseling theory. In the case of both Frankl and Skinner, the basic principles of their respective theories (on which their practices are constructed) are clearly referable back to the ontological, epistemological, and axiological precepts of humanism and environmentalism that were identified and discussed in the second major section of this text. The circular nature of this relationship is complete in the realization that the foundational principles of humanism and environmentalism are equally referable back to the ontological, epistemological and axiological precepts of metaphysics and antimetaphysics. The practices or techniques of counseling cannot exist without a theory of counseling to serve as a logical framework for those techniques. But at this point (and this is the point at which most counselors, theorists, counseling texts, and university counseling curriculums conclude) the relationship is still incomplete. To do total justice to their field, counseling practitioners and theorists must not only examine the theories that give birth to specific counseling practices, they must also examine the fundamental or meta-theories that give birth to specific counseling theories. The purpose of this text has been to attempt to identify and discuss the meta-theories (metaphysics and antimetaphysics) that serve as the foundations for general counseling theories (humanism and environmentalism) and specific counseling theorists (Frankl and Skinner), and to examine the necessary relationship between theorist, theory, and meta-theory.

It is the meta-theory that serves as the fundamental base or foundation on which sound counseling theories and practices can be built. But all too often this philosophic foundation is given either passing recognition or no recognition at all. Many within the field of counseling agree on the theoretical and practical principles of humanism and environmentalism. A random sampling of prestigious counseling texts illustrates this point. In looking at relatively recent books dedicated to a discussion of general counseling theory, a trend rapidly becomes apparent. These texts are in general agreement concerning the basic characteristics of environmentalism and humanism. The texts used in this random sample are as follows: Burks and Stefflre's *Theories of Counseling* (1979); Carkhuff and Berenson's *Beyond Counseling and Therapy* (1967); Corey's *Theory and Practice of Counseling Psychotherapy* (1977); Corsini's *Current Psychotherapies* (1973); Cunningham and Peter's *Counseling Theories* (1973); Patterson's *Theories of Counseling and Psychotherapy* (1980); Stefflre and Grant's *Theories of Counseling* (1972).

In terms of environmental theory, the texts discuss the same basic concepts. The concepts common to all the above texts are: biology and the environment serve as the crucial determinants of human behavior; the methods of the natural sciences (scientific method) concerning observability and verifiability of overt behavior are the only methods recognized; counseling in this manner is more or less value free in that it is undertaken to rid an individual of a specific symptom and anything that could be referred to as general value is merely the exercise of a society's will (a value is what society decides to call a value); all behavior is learned; no standard goal exists and treatment is relative; conditioning techniques and environmental manipulation (basically the same thing) are the behavior modification tools of the environmental "engineer"; humans are born as blank texts and are then shaped by environmental conditioning; humans have no innate nature; there is a great worth to humanity in laboratory experiments, including animal experiments, because of the continuity across the species. Not in this precise terminology, of course, but in almost every case each of the respective texts discusses these principles in addressing the topic of environmentalism.

The same commonality of basic humanistic characteristic is also present in these texts and can be seen in the following examples: humans are unique in the animal world; they are conscious of their own self-hood and are inner-directed by this self. Humans have the capability of transcendence of self; the subjective capacity of humankind is as important as scientific objectivity and many times even surpasses the objective realm because the phenomenological frame of reference of an individual is often the dominant frame of reference; the human self has an innate, essential nature (this point has been presented heretofore as a point of division between humanists in general and existentialists in particular. The existentialists have previously been shown to hold to the doctrine of existence before essence, no innate "inborn" nature for humanity is allowed in this view. This seems to create a logical conundrum for the existentialists because they do generally agree that humanity has the tendency of self-actualization, becoming the best self one can be. Where does this knowledge of one's best self come from unless it is inborn [innate]? If imposed by society, then it robs humanity of the unique ability to create one's own life in existence. If one does create one's own existence as the existentialists state, where does humanity get the mental picture of this best self that he/she is striving to reach? If he/she creates his/her own existence and has the tendency toward self-actualization [both points agreed upon by existentialists], then it seems logical that one has some innate structure "built in" to the self to serve as a guide for the attempt at self-actualization. Humanity must have some inborn idea of where it is going and what self-actualization is or else existence is merely a hit and miss proposition sanctioned by society. So at least, even in the existential branch of humanism, there is, implicitly, a recognition of the innate essential characteristics of humankind); values exist and if self-adjusted humanity will proceed to be the best it can be; humans have freedom and are responsible for the freedom of their choices; humanity creates as well as is created; problems arise when humans are alienated from the core of their being, their selves, and their fellow human selves.

It is easily recognized that the common characteristics briefly identified here from the aforementioned texts reveal a basic kinship to the fundamental precepts of ontology, epistemology, and axiology of humanism and environmentalism. This fact is obvious. But where to next? What subject is usually then broached by these texts after the outline of the basic theoretical concepts? In virtually every case there is an effort to show how these theoretical concepts influence and determine the practical techniques that are used in the actual work of the counselor. This is certainly not a fault in these texts because it provides much needed information on counseling's theoretical concepts and counseling's technical aspects. Also there is the constraint of literary practicality—one cannot cover every subject in every book. But this does leave some questions unanswered, the primary one being, where did the counseling theories come from that gave rise to the practices that accompany them? Certainly they represent the work of various counseling theorists, but the question persists, from where did the basic principles of the theories arise? In looking at the techniques, it is easy to infer a relationship between specific practices and specific theories. They fit together in a sense of "rightness." Is it possible, then, that if examined, the counseling theories might be found to fit together with specific meta-theories with a similar sense of rightness? Might, for example, this sense of rightness pervade all the way through metaphysics, general humanistic theory, Frankl's interpretation of that theory, and Frankl's implementation of those theories as counseling techniques? In this study this relationship certainly seems to be the case. To use the house analogy again, this relationship is important because without a strong foundation (the meta-theory) that is understood by the builders, the second stage of the house, the framework (the theory) is going to be constructed on a weak and shifting foundation, and the outside of the house (the practices and techniques) will be a preponderance of eclectic remedies formed upon a crumbling framework and founded on a poor and unfathomable foundation.

As the texts cited above indicate, there is a substantial amount of agreement concerning the theoretical constructs of humanism and environmentalism. This agreement continues into the area of practice and methodology. But would the agreement also be apparent when the philosophic principles undergirding the theories and practices are examined? This is the question that historically counseling has virtually ignored. The fundamental philosophic issues (meta-theory) in counseling present a wealth of material that could only move counseling in a positive direction if examined under the same rigorous standards applied to methodologies. Instead of questions of "what" or "how much" though, counseling would be examining itself by asking the question "why." Why does a behaviorist use conditioning techniques? Why does a humanist attempt to create a circumstance in which an individual can indulge his natural proclivity to be a better person? On the surface, these questions might appear to be matters of common sense, but this is not the case. These are difficult questions. They are philosophic questions, and the answers or paths to answers will be found only in a philosophic framework.

As in other fields of study, counseling uses (and perhaps overuses) linguistic labels as points of differentiation. One person claims to be a "Rogerian," another a "behaviorist," another an "existentialist," and so on. The point of division is not in the techniques used. One is not a behaviorist simply by using "successive approximation" or any other behavioral technique. Instead, a true behaviorist is one who is dedicated to a specific and particular set of philosophic principles. This philosophy of life is only complete when one is consciously aware of the principles that one follows. It also seems true to say, then, that counselors are only complete and at their best when they are consciously aware of the fundamental principles of being, knowing, and valuing upon which their theory and practices are built. In other words, counseling will truly progress when one knows and can explain *why* they are using successive approximation, not just *that* they are using this technique.

The alternative to a rational study of the philosophic principles of counseling is either Arbuckle's (1965) belief that counselors will be unaware of why they are doing what they are doing or Collingwood's (1940) belief that if one makes mistakes concerning fundamental principles then that mistake will quite likely infect all subsequent action with a certain amount of error. Obviously neither of these alternatives provides a sound foundation for the growth and betterment of counseling. On the other hand, though, a sound foundation is more likely when the area of counseling philosophy and its relationship to counseling theory and practice is recognized and studied in the literature, the college curriculum, and, most importantly, in each individual counselor's professional identity. This particular book takes only the smallest of steps in this direction. In examining the precepts of metaphysics and antimetaphysics and the relationship of these precepts to humanism and environmentalism in general and Frankl and Skinner in particular, this work makes the attempt to present key philosophic issues that exert specific influences on counseling theory and practice. The idea of a meta-theory is humanity's way of imposing a rational order from which specific theories are born. Those who feel that they can do just fine without such a philosophical base and even those who are opposed to such a philosophical base are already founding their beliefs on a vaguely defined philosophic base. It is unavoidable! There is no other way to decide what to believe or how to act. This antiphilosophical view is still derived from basic philosophic assumptions that are real and complex. "The ideas of antiphilosophers are more and not less likely to error in theory and practice because they are less openly expressed" (Stefflre & Grant, 1972, p. 3). Stated as simply as possible, this book has made an attempt to openly express the philosophic concerns that are essentially related to counseling theory and practice.

Trying to maintain a course dealing only with the main introductory (introductory in terms of counseling philosophy) categories resulted in two intellectual occurrences: One occurrence was the fact that no matter how introductory or general in nature this book tried to be, it was impossible not to raise some very important and very fascinating specific issues concerning counseling and philosophy along the way.

These issues were not always explicitly raised in the body of this paper, but certain ideas did implicitly bring these issues to mind. For example, the discussion of relative truth did not explicitly raise the issue of eclectic counseling theory, but it did imply this issue because eclecticism is logically founded on the principle of relativity. Many of the other issues were implied in this fashion rather than overtly stated; the second intellectual occurrence was the realization that these issues could not be adequately dealt with without dedicating one's life and thousands more pages to the attempt. So instead of pursuing each specific important issue as it presented itself, it seemed a better idea to adhere to the general introductory topics of concern and then to include some of the specific topics and a brief explanation of them in a closing section. The hope naturally being that others will find interest, fascination, and importance in these issues at some future time and will be able and willing to give them the attention they deserve.

Several of these specific issues were identified by Arbuckle (1958). He attempted to briefly touch upon issues commonly thought of as philosophical, that also had an impact on counseling. These issues, the self-concept; religion; the nature of man; counselor responsibility; and counselor education have all been touched upon in some small degree in this work. But an in-depth study of the heritage of these specific philosophical issues and the relationship between this philosophic heritage and the development of specific counseling theories and practices has not received the attention it deserves. There is one excellent glaring exception to this neglect. Colley's (1970) study of the counseling philosophy used just one of Arbuckle's philosophic issues, the nature of man, and studiously applied this issue to five specific counseling theories, the psychoanalytical approach, the rational (trait-factor) approach, the behavioral (environmental) approach, the phenomenological (client-centered) approach, and the existential approach. This work bridged the division between counseling and philosophy on this one issue. Despite this effort counseling still needs to expand its philosophic base. This present effort deals very briefly with the philosophic topic of God as logically implied in metaphysics and antimetaphysics, humanism and environmentalism. Also, Arbuckle (1958) identified religion as a key philosophic concept for counseling. Regardless of the obvious importance of the effect of God or religion on counselor, counseling theory, counselee, and counseling process, these effects have not been studied by counseling in any organized fashion in order to bring either philosophic or practical clarity to this relationship. Arbuckle (1958) emphasized the importance of this issue by asking, "to what extent, then, does one's religious philosophy, orientation, or bias act as a controlling agent, and affect the counselor's relationship with the client?" (p. 212). Put in another light, the question might perhaps be rephrased as follows: If Frankl's grandmother (as did Skinner's grandmother) had had him peer into the glowing coals in the stove and think on thoughts of hell and eternal damnation, would his view of God or religion be changed and more in tune with Skinner's view? One suspects that Skinner would agree that this would indeed be the case. From a Skinnerian point of view, the environment would bring certain contingencies of reinforcements to bear on a biologic subject and influence that subject to reflect this environmental heritage. Frankl would disagree with some parts of this assessment and stress that a self determining soul could view each experience (such as looking into glowing heater coals as a metaphor for hell) and freely decide what images to accept or reject. This would be based not only on an influencing cultural milieu but also on the implementation of one's personality theory from one's value system. These questions and speculations stem from the philosophic domain of counseling, and they need the same rigorous examination as that applied to other so-called "practical" aspects of counseling.

The idea of self-concept was again briefly touched upon by Arbuckle. Once more this is a philosophic issue as modern as today's news and, as of today, it is far from settled. In the October 10, 1983, issue of *Time* magazine, Skinner stated that "my parents' control was so well sustained that I had no chance to learn to revolt... I was never quite free. I never assumed I was not like my pigeons" (Skinner, cited by John Leo, 1983, p. 43). Yet in the same article it stated that a study by Norm Chomsky reached the conclusion that the structure of language was innate in human beings, and this idea does great damage to Skinner's theories (cited by John Leo, 1983). Also, psychologist Fergus Craik stated that, "we are not content to accept Skinner's dictum that there is nothing going on in there in the mind" (Craig, cited by John Leo, 1983, p. 43). It is obvious that this debate is nothing more than an up-to-date example of humanism versus environmentalism. The specific debate about the self-concept should be examined by counseling, and it should be examined in the light of the philosophic concepts that form its foundation.

In most counseling contexts the term self-concept usually has a double-edged meaning. It not only means how one sees oneself; it also means how one sees oneself with reference to others. Basically, it is a philosophy of life whereby a person defines oneself individually (to self) and also defines for the rest of society the position that one takes on various issues. If a counselor ignores the centuries old adage to "know thyself" (being consciously aware of the foundations that form the positions to be taken in life), then the stance one adopts on various theoretical or practical concerns will be unclear, both to self and others. When counseling theorists and practitioners exhibit a nonphilosophical viewpoint (actually, this is not possible; any nonphilosophical point of view is necessarily an antiphilosophical position), they exhibit an unsure foundation for both their theories and practices. This method foregoes the most important part of the meta-theory, theory, and practice triad of any thought process or application of that thought process. This lack of attention to the basic principles produces a discrepancy between what a counselor says he should do, what he believes he should do, and what he actually does in any given circumstance (Arbuckle, 1958). Often this discrepancy will not even be apparent to a particular practitioner. The discrepancy in counseling between what one says, what one believes, and what one does will only be apparent when one is aware of the fundamental principles that undergird what is said, believed, and practiced. Even then, though, just being aware of the discrepancy is not enough. Such discrepancies will disappear only when one commits oneself to a thorough examination of the philosophic principles that give birth to the specific theories and practices of a particular field of study. This is much more difficult than it sounds. Due to the amazing complexity of each individual, it is doubtful that one can ever truly know oneself. However, the effort to achieve this end inevitably moves one closer and closer to the goal, and enables one to more clearly define oneself and one's position to the rest of reality.

> This idea seems especially important to counselors because there seems to be some evidence to indicate that the counselor, as he actually works, is giving a display of his philosophy of life rather than showing how well he has learned certain techniques and procedures in a graduate school. (Arbuckle, 1958, p. 211)

In other words, counselors tend to implement their self-concepts through the choice of specific theories and practices employed in actual counseling encounters. The implementation of self-concepts through theoretical choice seems to fly somewhat in the face of eclecticism as a theoretical choice. What self-concept could be evidenced by selecting eclecticism as a counseling theory? What part of one's self would be implemented by choosing various theories for various clients? It does seem to pose something of a dilemma for the eclectic. Yet *The Personnel and Guidance Journal* (1983) listed two studies, by Garfield and Kurtz (1976) and by Smith (1982), and both found eclecticism to be on the rise.

In the Garfield study 55% of the clinical psychologists described themselves as eclectic and Smith found that 41% of clinical psychologists preferred to be called eclectic. Smith (1982) also noted that even though "eclecticism is clearly the preference of the largest number of psychologists, there seems to be dissatisfaction with the term" (p. 808).

> Without guidelines [a philosophical framework] to structure counseling and to govern the appropriate selection and application of theoretical demands, strategies, and techniques, the eclectic faces the danger of operating haphazardly [without philosophical structure] and inconsistently [without implementing a concept of self through theoretical choice], and less effectively than desirable. (Ward, 1983, p. 155)

If this is true (only further study along these philosophic lines can possibly answer this question), then it would seem to call into question the idea of eclecticism as the term is commonly used in counseling. Can there really be such an entity as a truly eclectic counselor? After all, pragmatic techniques and methods are only the tools used to achieve certain purposes. Conversely, goals and purposes can only be thought of as expressions of particular philosophic orientations (Arbuckle, 1958). Can one really employ techniques covering a broad spectrum of all those tools employed by various and conflicting counseling theories? What philosophic orientation would it imply to use one counseling tool based on humanistic theory one day and another tool based on environmental theory the next? These broad general theories are largely contradictory because the philosophic orientations that spawned them are largely contradictory. The first law of logic, of all rational thought, is the law of contradiction. If two thoughts are contradictory, one of them *must* be false. Therefore, can a counselor, who claims to have an eclectic approach, use various tools based on conflicting theories and conflicting philosophical orientations? The answer is, of course one can! But the important question is not *can* one, but *should* one, and what is the justification for doing so? The thread tying this work together is the idea of tracing humanistic ideas back to a foundational point of metaphysics and environmentalistic ideas back to a foundational point of antimetaphysics. With this in mind, where does eclecticism fit? To what foundational (or philosophical) point can this theory be traced? To be blunt, the answer is none! Eclecticism is a set of practices founded on many theories and based on no philosophical assumptions. When used from a strictly methodological point of view, eclecticism is easy to justify, but when one attempts to study the philosophical assumptions that give birth to these methods, one finds oneself at a dead end.

Eclecticism may work from a practical standpoint, but it cannot even exist from a philosophical standpoint because it has no consistent philosophical assumptions that undergird its methods. Without these philosophic assumptions, it would seem very easy for eclecticism to become bogged down in an inconsistent morass of random and purposeless technique. Only further study will answer the question, but it may be a truism that whatever theory or set of practices that one adopts, it merely represents the attempt to remain consistent with one's own self-concept. A person does not become a "Rogerian counselor" because a graduate course of study or certain professors influenced such a choice. Also, the choice is not made on the basis of random selection. In reality, one adopts a Rogerian stance because the fundamental principles of Rogers' ideas coincide with the fundamental beliefs of the individual. The choice of a counseling theory and a set of counseling practices reflects an attempt by each person to implement a view of one's self. This process can only occur when the individual "knows where he's coming from" in terms of the basic principles of being, knowing, valuing, and ultimacy. The alternative (not knowing where one is coming from) is a lack of self-knowledge, a lack of knowledge of one's own basic premises, an inconsistent approach to counseling (both theoretically and practically), and an ineffective career as a counselor. Such contradictory behavior is an improper approach and seems to portray counseling as a "bag of tricks" to be used on different occasions, in light of different situations. On the other hand, such a complete humanist as Viktor Frankl makes frequent use of environmental methods. What, then, is the difference? The difference seems to lie in the idea of being aware of a philosophic orientation and true to that orientation in the selection of goals for counseling and in the selection of tools to achieve those goals. When one is aware of philosophic foundations, and continually examines those personal foundations, and selects goals and methods that do not violate those foundations, then one is being aware of self and then the counseling discrepancies and contradictions concerning what one says, truly believes, and actually does will be, to some degree, eliminated. For example, once a counselor reaches the point where he/she has developed a fairly complete set of ontological beliefs and is also keenly aware of these beliefs, then that counselor will have a foundational concept of a view of human nature (i.e., humans are able/unable to solve their own problems). This single concept has an unbelievable ripple effect and helps to determine the counselor's selection of a theory, the selection of specific practices, even influencing such mundane decisions as physical posturing (in counseling sessions) and selection of office furniture. The point to be understood is the idea that each counselor should be aware of his or her own fundamental precepts before attempting to communicate on any level with others. The first step is to evaluate the idea of self-concept in terms of philosophic foundations and counseling concerns. This examination and understanding of personal fundamental beliefs is the cornerstone of all theoretical and practical counseling decisions.

Another philosophic issue that would easily lend itself to further study within the field of counseling is the idea of responsibility, especially counselor responsibility. In the final analysis, to whom is a counselor responsible: to self, to the client, or to society or some agent of society? The aspects of human freedom and human responsibility are examined in this study in the most general terms possible. Basically, freedom and responsibility are specific ideas derived from fundamental ontological and axiological premises. Again, it must be admitted that this is introductory material at best and, in truth, the issue of freedom and responsibility would by itself make an excellent specific subject for counseling to pursue in light of basic philosophic precepts. For example, this text deals only with the generalized oppositional character of whether or not humans are inner (self) directed. Can they exercise free choice and are they then responsible for these choices? Although it is the same dilemma, the problem seems to take on a more important aura when it is phrased in light of specific counselor situations. For example, does the counselor break the confidence of a teenaged client who has threatened imminent suicide? What is the counselor's responsibility in such a case? To whom are they responsible? Such a specific occurrence may call for action, but counselors who are aware of and who have examined their own philosophic orientations will at least address this issue of freedom and responsibility in terms that do not contradict or violate the fundamental principles guiding them in their own lives. The alternative is a very ineffective counselor.

> Since if the counselor himself does not have any concept of his role [which invariably means that he also has few concrete ideas about philosophic orientations] he will probably see no reason why he should not tell the principal about Mary's plans to run away, about Bobby's sexual deviations, about John's cheating in class. It is likely also, of course, that the number of his clients will rapidly decline and all those who do come in will be extremely wary and come forth with safe and innocuous statements. (Arbuckle, 1958, p. 213)

This is not meant to be an endorsement of total secrecy and of course there are other legal and ethical considerations that must serve as guidelines for the counselor. An example of such "practical" guidelines concerning counselor freedom and responsibility can be found in the "Ethical Principles of Psychologists," ("Ethical Principles of Psychologists," 1981). These principles have been established to provide the counselor with a legal and ethical structure designed to protect and aid both the counselor and the clientele. These principles give a basic structural framework concerning counselor freedom and responsibility. The point to be made about this issue, though, is the same thread that permeates each phase of this text. The point is that these practical principles governing freedom and responsibility are themselves derived from some philosophical position or some meta-theory. This is evident in the preamble of these principles. The opening passage of this document demands that psychologists (and counselors) respect the dignity and worth of the individual and also preserve and protect fundamental human rights. It is obvious that the attempt to adopt these precepts into one's own code of behavior necessitates that each counselor must evaluate the terms "fundamental human rights" and individual "worth and dignity" according to a basic philosophy of life. This study has looked generally at two such basic philosophies (antimetaphysics/environmentalism and metaphysics/humanism) but much work needs to be done in order to evaluate specific issues in counseling, such as responsibility and freedom, not just according to legal or ethical considerations only (although those are certainly important), but also according to the basic philosophical concerns on which people build their lives. Often the legal and ethical principles do not completely satisfy a counselor's specific problem, and it is at this point that a counselor needs to indulge in self-examination to isolate those fundamental principles that form the cornerstones of his/her life and then apply these principles, along with legal and ethical precepts, to try to arrive at the right solution to any given problem. Being unaware of one's own fundamental philosophical beliefs forbids such a process and makes specific issues in counseling that much more difficult to solve. Sometimes there is no practical solution to a practical problem. The solutions are only found in the ethical and legal guidelines and in the counselor's philosophic orientation toward freedom, responsibility, and other specific issues. In this case, as in most others, the most practical thing in the world is a well thought out purpose for life founded on one's carefully examined philosophic foundations.

Another important issue concerns the idea of counselor education. Skinner said that environmentalism "is the method of the analysis of behavior, which, I think, has no rival at the moment. It has completely displaced all of the other ways of studying behavior" (Skinner, cited by John Leo, 1983, p. 43). It seems fair to say that there is some justification to this statement. There does seem to be a distinct environmental slant to a majority of counselor education curriculums. Does this mean that the students will automatically become environmentalists? Although more work is necessary in this area to accurately judge the effect of a teacher's (counselor) philosophic orientation on the later philosophic orientation of those students under his/her tutelage, it seems likely that students do not automatically adopt a teacher or a counseling program's philosophic orientation. A study by Arbuckle and Wicas (1957) indicated that

> counselors receiving their doctorate education from one institution appear to differ in their attitudes and their techniques of counseling in just as many ways as those receiving their professional preparation in many different institutions. (Arbuckle, 1958, p. 211)

As he (1958) noted, "perhaps the question for the counselor-educator is not what does the student know, but rather what can he do with what he knows?" (p. 214). Not just what technique can one use, but what rational thought process has occurred to allow the student a chance to construct a clear, concise, and consistent philosophic framework for the techniques applied in practice? The only way to reach such an institutional goal is to promote counseling philosophy as an equal partner of counseling theory and technique. In this way, future counselors can examine philosophical issues and engage in self-analysis in the light of these issues and emerge as a better counselor for the experience.

Colley (1970) and others have pointed out still another area dealing with the relationship of philosophy to counseling that needs further study. The question raised is this: to what extent are the metatheories, theories, and practices adopted by specific counseling theorists a result of the cultural and environmental milieu of that theorist? Is each theorist merely writing out of the "spirit of his time" or is the theorist indulging in a sense of rebellion against the spirit of his time or does this idea affect specific theorists at all? It is indeed difficult to believe the latter view. For example, how many of Skinner's theories could be envisioned without remembering the determined structure of his immediate household. Also what parts of his theories bear the imprint of the influence of the progress of science in the industrial revolution, and the continued advent of Darwin's naturalistic teachings, Dewey's instrumentalism, Pavlov, Watson, and the logical positivist philosophers. Equally, one cannot envision Freud separated from Victorianism and Calvinism, or Rogers from his neo-orthodox heritage, or Frankl separated from his death camp experiences. What part do these environmental and experiential brush strokes play in painting the canvases of the lives of these great thinkers who so influenced counseling? These subjects need to be examined by counseling as a part of the necessary self-examination that all fields of study must undergo. There are so many other topics to be examined. This book has attempted to look "broadly" at two general philosophical positions of opposition in counseling. But what about other specific theories? For instance, what are the precise philosophical assumptions on which Rational Emotive Therapy are constructed? What are the epistemological concerns of Miller and Dollard's theory? What specific axiological presuppositions form the foundations of Rogers' Person-Centered theory? The questions are virtually endless and the task is formidable. But for continued growth and prosperity, counseling must be more considerate of its philosophic heritage, and it must examine this heritage with the same exacting standards used to study counseling methodology and counseling theory.

> Counseling is an expression of human values and human attitudes, and as the counselor is working..., he is giving a fairly clear picture of his own personal philosophical concept of man, his nature, and his function on earth. It would seem logical that the first question that should be examined is the question why... The "why" is the philosophical rationale for whatever one does as a counselor. (Arbuckle, 1965, p. 3)

At some point in one's professional life this "why" question must be dealt with if counseling is to progress as a worthwhile field of study. Examining this why must be undertaken along two lines. First, counseling as a profession must rid itself of its penchant for immediacy in problem solving and must indulge in a philosophical examination of itself as a field of study and arrive at some basic conclusions concerning the ends it seeks to achieve, its goals, its methods, and its overall "place" in the scientific community. Secondly, this philosophical self-examination should be practiced on an individual level by each member of the counseling community. Only in this way will counseling be able to compose a stable set of consistent ontological, epistemological, and axiological points of view. Only then will individual counselors adopt a self-consistent stance on being, knowing, and valuing that will enhance their status as counselors and even more importantly will enable them to provide positive and purposeful services to those who seek their help.

Bibliography

Allport, G. W. (1955). *Becoming*. New Haven, CT: Yale University Press.

Allport, G. W. (1961). *Patterns of growth in personality*. New York: Holt, Rinehart and Winston.

Arbuckle, D. W. (1958). Five philosophical issues in counseling. *Journal of Counseling Psychology*, 5, 211-215.

Arbuckle, D. S. (1965). *Counseling: Philosophy, theory, and practice*. Boston: Allyn and Bacon.

Arbuckle, D. W., & Wicas, E. (1957). The development of a counseling perception instrument. *Journal of Counseling Psychology*, 4, 304-312.

Ayer, A. J. (1945). *Language, truth, and logic* (lst ed.). New York: Dover Publications.

Ayer, A. J. (1946). *Language, truth, and logic* (2nd ed.). New York: Dover Publications.

Ayer, A. J. (1968). *The origins of pragmatism*. San Francisco: Freeman, Cooper and Co., 1968.

Barclay, J. R. (1968). *Counseling and philosophy: A theoretical exposition*. Boston: Houghton Mifflin.

Barclay, J. R. (1971). *Foundations of counseling strategies*. New York: John Wiley and Sons.

Barrett, C. (1935). *Philosophy*. New York: Macmillan.

Beck, C. E. (1963). *Philosophical foundations of guidance*. Englewood Cliffs, NJ: Prentice-Hall.

Bradley, F. H. (1908). *Appearance and reality*. New York: Macmillan.

Brentano, F. (1902). *Origin of the knowledge of right and wrong* (C. Hague and A. Constable, Trans.). London: Westminster Press.

Brubacher, J. S. (1965). *Bases for policy in higher education*. New York: McGraw-Hill.

Burks, H. M., & Stefflre, B. (1979). *Theories of counseling*. New York: McGraw-Hill.

Butler, J. D. (1951). *Four philosophies and their practice in education and religion*. New York: Harper and Brothers.

Butler, J. D. (1966). *Idealism in education*. New York: Harper and Row.

Carkhuff, R. R., & Berenson, B. G. (1967). *Beyond counseling and therapy*. New York: Holt, Rinehart and Winston.

Carnap, R. (1953). *The logical syntax of language*. New York: Humanities Press.

Carnap, R. (1956). The methodological character of theoretical concepts. In H. Feigl & M. Scriven (Eds.), *Minnesota studies in the philosophy of science.* Minneapolis: University of Minnesota Press.

Carnap, R. (1957). The elimination of metaphysics. In A. J. Ayer (Ed.), *Logical positivism.* New York: Free Press of Glencoe.

Carnap, R. (1959). Psychological in physical language. In A. J. Ayer (Ed.), *Logical positivism.* New York: Glencoe Free Press.

Colley, S. (1973). An examination of five major movements in counseling theory in terms of how representative theorists view the nature of man (Doctoral dissertation, University of Alabama, 1970). *Dissertation Abstracts International, 31,* lOA-A. (University Microfilms No. 71-09071)

Collingwood, R. G. (1940). *An essay on metaphysics.* Oxford: Clarendon Press.

Copleston, F. C., S. J. (1962). A realist's rejoinder. In D. A. Drennen (Ed.), *A modern introduction to metaphysics.* New York: The Free Press.

Corey, G. (1977). *Theory and practice of counseling psychotherapy.* Belmont, CA: Wadsworth.

Creighton, J. E. (1929). The social nature of thinking. In D. S. Robinson (Ed.), *An anthology of recent philosophy.* New York: Thomas Y. Crowell.

Cribben, J. (1951). *An analysis of the theological, philosophical, psychological, and sociological principles of guidance presented in textbooks published since 1935.* New York: Fordham University.

Cunningham, L. M., & Peters, H. J. (1973). *Counseling theories: A selective examination for school counselors.* Columbus, OH: Charles E. Merrill.

Descartes, R. (1964). From mediation V. In J. Hick (Ed.), *The existence of God.* New York: Macmillan.

Dewey, J. (1916). *Democracy and education.* New York: Macmillan.

Drennen, D. A. (1962). *A modern introduction to metaphysics.* New York: The Free Press.

Ethical principles of psychologists. (1981). *American Psychologist, 36,* 633-638.

Feibleman, J. K. (1960). *An introduction to Peirce's philosophy: Interpreted as a system.* London: George Allen and Unwin.

Frankl, V. (1955). *Man and meaning.* New York: A. A. Knopf.

Frankl, V. (1959). *Man's search for meaning: An introduction to logotherapy.* Boston: Beacon Press.

Frankl, V. (1967). *Psychotherapy and existentialism: Selected papers on logotherapy.* New York: Simon and Schuster.

Frankl, V. (1969). *The will to meaning: Foundations and applications of logotherapy.* Cleveland, OH: World.

Frankl, V. (1973). *The doctor and the soul: From psychotherapy to logotherapy.* New York: Random House.

Frankl, V. (1975). *The unconscious God: Psychotherapy and theology.* New York: Simon and Shuster.

Garfield, S. L., & Kurtz, L. (1976). A survey of clinical psychologists: Characteristics, activities, and orientation. *The Clinical Psychologist, 28,* 7-10.

Gilson, E. (1937). *The unity of philosophical experience.* New York: Charles Scribner's Sons.

Goldstein, A. (1973). Behavior therapy. In R. Corsini (Ed.), *Current psychotherapies.* Itasca, IL: Peacock Publishers

Gould, J. A. (1975). Of what does knowledge consist? In J. Gould (Ed.), *Classical philosophical questions.* Columbus, OH: Charles E. Merrill.

Harris, T. G. (1971). The B. F. Skinner manifesto: An introduction. *Psychology Today,* 5(3), 33-36.

Hitt, W. (1969). Two models of man. *American Psychologist, 24,* 651-657.

Hocutt, M. (1980). *First philosophy: An introduction to philosophical issues.* Belmont, CA: Wadsworth.

Hoernle, A. (1927). *Idealism as a philosophy.* Chicago: George H. Doran.

Holy Bible. New York: Oxford University Press, n.d.

Hume, D. (1912). *An inquiry concerning human understanding and selection from a treatise of human nature.* Open Court, Chicago:

Hutchins, R. M. (1936). *The higher learning in America.* New Haven, CT: Yale University Press.

Hutchins, R. M. (1943). *Education for freedom.* Baton Rouge: Louisiana State University Press.

James, W. (1909). *The meaning of truth.* New York: Longmans, Green.

Kanfer, F. H., & Phillips, J. S. (1970). *Learning foundations of behavior therapy.* New York: Wiley.

Kant, I. (1938). *The fundamental principles of the metaphysics of ethics* (0. Manthey-Zorn, Trans.). New York: D. Appleton-Century.

Kemp, C. G. (1971). Existential counseling. *The Counseling Psychologist,* 2(3), 2-29.

Kierkegaard, S. (1954). *Fear and trembling* (W. Lowrie, Trans.). New York: Doubleday.

Koch, S. (1964). Psychology and emerging conceptions of knowledge as unitary. In T. W. Wann (Ed.), *Behaviorism and phenomenology: Contrasting bases for modern psychology*. Chicago: The University of Chicago Press.

Krikorian, Y. W., & Edel, A. (1959). *Contemporary philosophic problems*. New York: Macmillan.

Kulpe, 0. (1897). *Introduction to philosophy*. London: Swan Sonnenschein.

Kung, H. (1978). *Does God exist: An answer for today* (E. Quinn, Trans.). New York: Doubleday.

Lazerowitz, M. (1955). *The structure of metaphysics*. London: Routledge, and Kegan Paul.

Leo, J. (1983). Still working faster and longer. *Time, 122*(16), 42-43.

Lewis, C. S. (1973). *The problem of pain*. New York: Macmillan.

MacLeod, R. B. (1964). Phenomenology: A challenge to experimental psychology. In T. W. Wann (Ed.), *Behaviorism and phenomenology: Contrasting bases for modern psychology*. Chicago: The University of Chicago Press.

Malcolm, N. (1964). Behaviorism as a philosophy of psychology. In T. W. Wann (Ed.), *Behaviorism and phenomenology: Contrasting bases for modern psychology*. Chicago: The University of Chicago Press.

Maritain, J. (1939). *A preface to metaphysics*. New York: Sheed and Ward.

May, R. (1967). *Psychology and the human dilemma*. Princeton, NJ: D. Van Nostrand.

May, R., Angel, E., & Ellenberger, H. F. (1958). *Existence*. New York: Basic Books.

Michael, J., & Meyerson, L. (1962). A behavioral approach to counseling and guidance. *Harvard Educational Review, 32*(4), 382-402.

Misiak, H., & Sexton, V. W. (1973). *Phenomenological, existential, and humanistic psychologies: A historical survey*. New York: Grune and Stratton.

Moore, G. E. (1925). A defense of common sense. In J. H. Muirhead (Ed.), *Contemporary British philosophy*. New York: Macmillan.

Mullen, J. D. (1981). *Kierkegaard's philosophy: Self deception and cowardice in the present age*. New York: New American Library.

Oppenheimer, R. (1956). Analogy in science. *American Psychologist, 11*, 58.

Paley, W. (1964). Natural theology. In J. Hick (Ed.), *The existence of God*. New York: Macmillan.

Patterson, C. H. (1980). *Theories of counseling and psychotherapy*. New York: Harper and Row.

Peirce, C. S. (1953). Pragmatism and meaning. In C. Hartshorne & P. Weiss (Eds.), *Collected papers of Charles Sanders Peirce*. Cambridge: Harvard University Press.

Peirce, C. S. (1955). How to make our ideas clear. In J. Buckler (Ed.), *Philosophical writings of Peirce*. New York: Dover.

Peirce, C. S. (1966). The fixation of belief. In P. Wiener (Ed.), *Charles S. Peirce: Selected writings*. New York: Dover.

Plato. (1972). *The dialogues* (4 vols.) (B. Jowett, Trans.). New York: Charles Scribner's Sons.

Popkin, R. H., & Stroll, A. (1956). *Philosophy made simple*. Garden City, NY: Doubleday.

Riska, A. (1972). Methodology and philosophy. *Metaphilosophy*, 3(3), 219-237.

Rogers, C. R. (1963). Psychotherapy for today or where do we go from here? *American Journal of Psychotherapy*, *17*, 15-16.

Rogers, C. R. (1964). Toward a science of the person. In T. W. Wann (Ed.), *Behaviorism and phenomenology: Contrasting bases for modern psychology*. Chicago: The University of Chicago Press.

Royce, J. (1919). *Lectures on modern idealism*. New Haven: Yale University Press.

Sartre, J. P. (1947). *Existentialism* (B. Rechtman, Trans.). New York: Philosophical Library.

Schmitt, R. (1967). Phenomenology. In P. Edwards (Ed.), *The encyclopedia of philosophy* (vol. 6). New York: Macmillan.

Scriven, M. (1964). Views of human nature. In T. W. Wann (Ed.), *Behaviorism and phenomenology: Contrasting bases for modern psychology*. Chicago: The University of Chicago Press.

Skinner, B. F. (1948). *Walden Two*. New York: Macmillan.

Skinner, B. F. (1953). *Science and human behavior*. New York: Macmillan.

Skinner, B. F. (1964). Behaviorism at fifty. In T. W. Wann (Ed.), *Behaviorism and phenomenology: Contrasting bases for modern psychology*. Chicago: The University of Chicago Press, 1964.

Skinner, B. F. (1971a). Beyond freedom and dignity. *Psychology Today*, 5(3), 37-83.

Skinner, B. F. (1971b). *Beyond freedom and dignity*. New York: A. A. Knopf.

Skinner, B. F. (1976). *About behaviorism*. New York: Random House, 1976.

Smith, D. (1982). Trends in counseling and psychotherapy. *American Psychologist*, *37*, 802-809.

Soltis, J. F. (1978). *An introduction to the analysis of educational concepts*. Reading, MA: Addison-Wesley.

Spiegelberg, H. (1960). *The phenomenological movement: A historical introduction* (2 vols.). The Hague, Netherlands: Martinus Nijhoff.

Staats, A. W., & Staats, C. K. (1963). *Complex human behavior*. New York: Holt, Rinehart and Winston.

St. Anselm. (1964). The ontological argument. In J. Hick (Ed.), *The existence of God*. New York: Macmillan.

Stefflre, B., & Grant, W. H. (1972). *Theories of counseling*. New York: McGraw-Hill.

Taylor, A. E. (1903). Elements of metaphysics. London: Methuen.

Taylor, A. E. (1926). The vindication of religion. In E. G. Selwyn (Ed.), *Essays catholic and critical*. New York: Macmillan.

Taylor, A. E. (1964). The argument from religious experience. In J. Hick (Ed.), *The existence of God*. New York: Macmillan.

Thevenaz, P. (1962). *What is phenomenology?* Chicago: Quadrangle Books.

Ullman, L. P., & Krasner, L. A. (1969). *approach to abnormal behavior*. Englewood Cliffs, NJ: Prentice-Hall.

Urban, W. M. (1930). Metaphysics and value. In G. P. Adams & W. P. Montague (Eds.), *Contemporary American philosophy* Vol. 2). New York: Macmillan.

Walsh, W. H. (1967). Nature of metaphysics. In P. Edwards (Ed.), *The encyclopedia of philosophy* (Vol. 5). New York: Macmillan.

Ward, D. E. (1983). The trend toward eclecticism and the development of comprehensive models to guide counseling and psychotherapy. *Journal of Personnel and Guidance, 62*(3), 154-157.

Watson, J. B. (1916). The place of the conditioned reflex in psychology. *Psychological Review, 23*, 89-116.

Watson, J. B. (1924). *Psychology from the standpoint of a behaviorist* (2nd ed.). Philadelphia: Lippincott.

Weitzman, B. (1967). Behavior therapy and psychotherapy. *Psychological Review, 74*, 300-317.

Wittgenstein, L. (1922). *Tractatus logico-hilosophicus*. New York: Harcourt, Brace.

White, L. (1978). Theoretical orientations of counselor educators. *Journal of College Student Personnel, 19*(2), 132-135.

White, M. G. (1943). The origins of Dewey's *instrumentalism*. New York: Columbia University Press.

Whitehead, A. N. (1962). Method and theory. In D. A. Drennen (Ed.), *A modern introduction to metaphysics*. New York: The Free Press.

Wilson, J. (1969). *Language and the pursuit of truth*. New York: Cambridge University Press.

Yates, A. J. (1970). *Behavior therapy.* New York: Wiley.

Yolton, J. W. (1967). *Metaphysical analysis.* Toronto: University of Toronto Press.

Yolton, J. W. (1980). Hume's ideas. In J. W. Davis (Ed.), *Hume Studies,* 6 1), 1-25.

Zax, N., & Klein, A. (1960). Measurement of personality and behavior changes following psychotherapy. *Psychological Bulletin, 57,* 38.